Botany, Ballet & Dinner from Scratch

The chapter *Raspberry Cordial* originally appeared as *Memory, preserved...* in the November 2007 issue of Culinate.com.

Heliotrope Books LLC
heliotropebooks@gmail.com

Cover Photograph by Richard Orbach
Designed and Typeset by Naomi Rosenblatt with AJ&J Design

Botany, Ballet & Dinner from Scratch:

A Memoir with Recipes

Leda Meredith

Heliotrope Books

New York City

To dancer Penelope Lagios Coberly, my mom,

To pianist Kelly Johnson, my dad,

And in memory of Paul G. Varni

❧ *Table of Contents* ❧

ALSO BY LEDA MEREDITH:

The Forager's Feast: How to Identify, Gather, and Prepare Wild Edibles, W.W. Norton, 2016

Preserving Everything: Can, Culture, Pickle, Freeze, Ferment, Dehydrate, Salt, Smoke, and Store Fruits, Vegetables, Meat, Milk, and More, W.W. Norton, 2014

Northeast Foraging: 120 Wild and Flavorful Edibles from Beach Plums to Wineberries, Timber Press, 2014

The Locavore's Handbook: The Busy Person's Guide to Eating Local on a Budget, Globe Pequot Press, 2010

❧ *Foreword to the New Edition* ❧

I was so delighted when my publisher asked me to do an updated, annotated version of this book. My first thoughts were along the lines of "Yippee! I can add more recipes, and update the local food movement info" (so much has changed for the better since I wrote this book!), and "I can let people know about the other sustainable food systems books I've written since, and..."

Well, this is a memoir, after all. I guess I should let you know that I am now married to the wonderful man I wrote about in the Mint Tea & a Ride Not Taken chapter. When I wrote that chapter, I hadn't seen him in almost twenty years, and I had no idea that we'd ever meet again.

Oh, and I moved to another continent to be with him. Sort of.

Whew.

So here's what I ended up doing with this opportunity to revisit *Botany, Ballet, & Dinner from Scratch*:

There are new recipes.

There are thoughts about where the sustainable food movement has succeeded and where it still has a long way (and not much time) to go.

There are personal updates and random musings along the way. And this time, there are photos.

I hope you will enjoy both reading this new version of my first book and cooking from it.

—Leda

❧ *Introduction* ❧

Leda Meredith changed my life.

I know that sounds like an exaggeration, delivered for dramatic effect, but it's the truth. Leda and I met in a medical botany class at the New York Botanical Garden. We shared class notes and the occasional subway ride home. For the next few years she worked for me as the foreman of my Acme Plant Stuff gardening crew. When we'd break for lunch, Leda would pick a few leaves of garlic mustard from a weedy part in the garden and stick them in her sandwich. Did I think that was weird? Yes. But interesting.

She talked endlessly about CSAs (Community Supported Agriculture), foraging, and food preservation, and I began to understand why these things made sense, focusing on homemade, local, seasonal foods. She fed me tidbits of gingko nut pesto and spicebush ice cream, and I couldn't argue with the unusual, distinctive tastes. I swallowed the bait and asked for more.

If you're reading this introduction, then you, too, have taken the bait; you're in for a delicious and fascinating ride. In *Botany, Ballet, and Dinner from Scratch* Leda has collected some of her most personal recipes. Placing these recipes in the context of her life as a dancer, gardener, and forager, gives them special significance.

When Leda explains the scrapes on her arms to Cynthia Gregory at a glitzy NYC ballet fundraiser, she takes us back to a citrus grove in Southern Greece, where just a few days earlier she picked oranges to earn her airfare back to the states. Battling rain, gypsies, and sharp thorns, Leda triumphs, and finishes the chapter with a recipe for Peloponnese chicken with oranges. It's an unexpected flavor combination: sweet and tart, with a blend of spices that evokes the Mediterranean.

If you love food, love to cook, and believe it's important to have a personal relationship with your food, this book is for you. If you want to make home-grown, home-cooked food an essential part of your life, but aren't sure how to get started, this book is for you. If you're simply curious about how a professional ballet dancer traveled around the world and ended up teaching classes on wild edibles in the Bronx, this book is for you.

Leda is a passionate and accomplished teacher; her clear, well-written recipes are easy to follow and sound so delicious, you'll want to try them all. As you follow her journey and try her recipes, you'll certainly be inspired. Perhaps to cook, perhaps to forage, perhaps to write your own story.

— Ellen Zachos

UPDATE: ...and I'm delighted to report that I did such an excellent job of hooking Ellen on foraging that she not only became an expert forager but went on to write an excellent book on the subject, *Backyard Foraging: 65 Familiar Plants You Didn't Know You Could Eat (Storey Publishing, March 2013).*

Part One: Blackberry Hill

❧ Yia-Yia's Horta ❧

I lived with my great-grandmother, my grandmother, and sometimes my mother across the street from the park and a short drive from the ocean. We lived in a city, San Francisco, but most of my early memories happened on sand or under trees. Of the house we lived in, I only remember one of the rooms: the kitchen.

Every spring there came a moment when Yia-Yia Lopi, my great-grandmother, stubbed out her Kool menthol cigarette and declared that it was the right day to gather *horta* in the park. The timing had to be just right: too soon and the leaves would be too small, too late and they'd be bitter. Yia-Yia was the expert on when to go because she'd grown up picking wild edible greens in Greece. I was her assistant. We stuffed our plastic shopping bags with dandelion greens, wild mustard, and *Claytonia*. I don't remember her teaching me to identify plants the way I teach my students now, pointing out leaf margins and other botanical details. I remember her rolling her eyes impatiently if I brought her the wrong leaves, and I remember trying not to repeat that mistake because her disapproving silence frightened me.

Back in the kitchen, Yia-Yia told me to stay out of the way. I watched as she and Grandma Nea washed the leaves with obvious glee, both of them speaking at once in rapid-fire Greek. Then they stirred the steaming greens, added chopped garlic, and poured in olive oil. Their eyes would gleam in anticipation of a favorite treat. The first wild greens of spring were better to them than chocolate, or at least as good.

My Grandma Nea was a kindergarten teacher. She taught me to read and loved taking me to the beach. She took me seriously when I told her that the raindrops on the car window were talking to me. Sometimes when my mom was home the two of them would argue, long fights in the kitchen that I didn't understand except that I heard my name a lot and *L.A., home, dance, father*.

Yia-Yia Lopi was widowed, Grandma Nea divorced, and my mom, Penelope, was dancing with a ballet company in L.A. She tells me that she tried to keep me with her but my grandmothers took me away because a dance company "wasn't a good environment for a child."

I don't remember her absences as clearly as I remember saving crusts of bread in a bag near the stove. When Mom came back to San Francisco we fed the crusts to ducks on a pond in the park. I pointed out which greens I'd picked with Yia-Yia, and Mom hugged me until I squirmed. Then we started walking. Mom had a knack for getting lost, and Golden Gate Park is big enough and wild enough that you can indeed get lost in it. We never took the paved paths, preferring the dirt trails that wound between the trees. I collected eucalyptus pods shaped like acorns, perfect pebbles, daisy chains that broke but were too pretty to leave behind. It was easy to pretend I was in a real, wild wood with my mother rather than just a park across the street from Grandma's house. If we got very lost it could be hours before we had to go home.

Me, Mom, and Grandma Nea

UPDATE: Grandma Nea lived long enough to read my second book, which was dedicated to her (*The Locavore's Handbook: The Busy Person's Guide to Eating Local on a Budget*). She passed away a few weeks after her 99th birthday, still humming tunes and curious about the world.

Yia-Yia's Horta (Greens Greek-Style)
Serves 4

This recipe is so basic that I almost didn't include it. But then I thought about all the recipes my great-grandmother knew that I never learned because she thought they were too obvious to bother teaching. The know-how of so many excellent home cooks has been lost because nobody wrote it down. Each generation expected the next to learn what they knew as they had learned it, but recent generations were just trying to leave the past behind and didn't pass their knowledge on.

There are two recipes for leafy greens here: one is Yia-Yia's version, and one is a variation that I use just as often. They are methods more than recipes, and I encourage you to experiment and come up with your own variations. But first, here is how we liked our horta, *our wild spring greens, when we were four generations of women living between an ocean and a park:*

1 large bunch dandelion, mustard, or other leafy greens (whether foraged or store-bought these will be at their best only in the spring and fall. In summer they are too bitter.)
Extra-virgin olive oil
2 cloves garlic, peeled and minced (more is good, too)
Juice of 1 lemon
Salt

1. Bring an inch of water to a boil in a large pot. Add the greens a little at a time, stirring them down into the liquid as they wilt. Once they are all wilted, let them simmer 5 to 10 minutes, stirring occasionally. When the greens are tender, turn off the heat.

2. Lift the greens out with tongs and place in a heap on a plate. Squeeze the lemon juice over the greens and stir in the garlic. Add salt to taste. Drizzle some good quality extra-virgin olive oil on top. Serve at room temperature.

* My Grandma Nea (95 at the time of this writing) just called to remind me that she always drinks the cooking liquid because it is good for you.

Greens Another Way
Serves 4

Same ingredients, different method:

1 large bunch dandelion, mustard, or other leafy greens
2 tablespoons extra-virgin olive oil
2 cloves garlic, peeled and minced
Juice of 1 lemon
Salt

1. Wash but do not dry the greens. Add them a little at a time to a large skillet over medium heat. As the leaves wilt you will be able to fit more in. If necessary, add a small amount of water to prevent sticking.

2. When all of the greens are wilted and tender but still bright green, add the minced garlic and one tablespoon of the olive oil. Stir for 2 minutes more to lightly cook the garlic. Serve warm or at room temperature with the lemon juice and remaining olive oil drizzled over the top and salt if desired.

Where It Comes From

I spent my 5th birthday on a rocky beach in my grandfather's Greek village. My mom and I had been in Europe for nine months. There is a photo of me taken the morning we left San Francisco: I am sitting on a suitcase surrounded by the rest of our luggage, clutching a wrought iron fence and peering through it at the camera with a no-nonsense, ready-for-anything expression.

We went to Germany first. That winter was one of the coldest on record, so brutal that frozen birds dropped out of the trees, once onto the pavement in front of me. My mother was trying to get a dance job. Auditioning for ballet companies with a four year old in tow wasn't practical, and she couldn't afford a babysitter, so she put me in an orphanage temporarily. This was almost as awful as it sounds. I didn't speak German and no one there spoke English. The big room where we kids slept, all our beds in a row, was cold and so was the cafeteria. The food was heavy and starchy and bland. When I didn't finish everything on my plate a woman with a perpetual frown and a double chin would sit down next to me and force-feed me. She was not gentle: I still remember how the tines of the fork felt when they scraped the back of my throat.

By the end of a month, my mom had gotten a contract with the opera ballet in Augsburg. When she came to pick me up, Ms. Double Chin brought me to the front door to meet her. Mom didn't recognize me at first. I had gone from being a skinny kid with long tangled hair to a little stranger with tight braids on either side of recently fattened cheeks. She looked right past me eagerly, waiting for her daughter to appear. Then she looked back at me and her eyebrows flew up in surprise as she realized who I was.

I didn't know why we left Germany after just a few months, but I was glad. We headed south, my mom turning each step of the journey into a game. I took being a world-traveler seriously and didn't appreciate her attempts to be cheerful. I have a vivid memory of sitting in a cafe at a train station in Milan. "Mom," I said, "Our train is going to leave."

"No, honey, it's not for another hour."

"No, mom, it's now."

I was right and we missed our train, which was the last one that day. We spent the night being driven around by a taxi driver. I didn't appreciate that I was warm and could sleep on the soft back seat of the car instead of on a hard bench at the station. I was too busy being mad at her.

From Italy we went to Cannes. Mom told me the money was running out, and that was why we ate the same meal every day for two weeks straight: baguettes and salad. I didn't mind. I loved it there. The air was warm, the bread was chewy and crusty and good, and there was a huge honeysuckle vine outside. I loved to sip the drop of sweet nectar each flower held. By the time we left France I once again looked like the knobby-kneed, wild-haired kid my mom recognized as her daughter.

Once the money was really, *really* gone Mom called Papou, my grandfather, in Greece. He bailed us out and we spent most of the next year in his village of Paralia Sergoulas. For my 5th birthday, my great-aunt Zoitsa baked an enormous cake in her wood oven. She and Papou's second wife, Nikolitsa, made enough moussaka to serve the whole village. Papou had invited everyone to his granddaughter's party. "Everyone" didn't add up to more than 15 people from the village, but I was still impressed.

I befriended the neighbor's lamb. I visited it everyday, stopping to reach through the wooden fence. It would butt its curly head up under my hand. Nobody bothered to tell me that my pet was destined to be dinner, probably because that seemed too obvious to bother mentioning.

I was present for the slaughter, and it is true what they say about the silence of the lambs. This one didn't make a sound. It just looked up at the neighbor's wife with trusting, puzzled eyes as she pulled its head back with one hand while the other hand slashed a knife horizontally. Brilliant red blood gushed in a line across the curly wool. I ran back to my grandfather's house screaming that they were all murderers. My grandfather told me I was being ridiculous. I hollered back that I was never speaking to any of them ever, ever again and declared myself a vegetarian. I was from California, and even at five years old knew what a vegetarian was, more or less. My vegetarianism didn't last long, but the impact of seeing that lamb butchered did. I wanted to know exactly where everything on my plate came from.

I still get quite heated about the importance of acknowledging where my food comes from. To me it is even more important than whether or not the food is stamped with a politically correct organic certification. Yes, organically grown and fed food causes less environmental damage than conventional agribusiness farming. Yes, such food is often higher in nutritional value. Yes, it tastes better. Yes, yes, yes…but the real point, to me, is that this food was alive and now it is about to become…me. Yet in a very basic sense I am a hypocrite on this subject because in over forty years of eating meat I have never killed an animal for food. I am not proud of that fact.

My friends and I like to think we're fairly enlightened about our food choices. We've read Pollan's *The Omnivore's Dilemma* and other bibles of the sustainable agriculture movement. We shop at the farmers' markets and the words "local" and "seasonal" have become our mantras. But we were raised without exposure to messiness and death. If asked, most of us would agree that the way indigenous peoples used every part of a hunted animal out of need and respect was better than our mass-produced and packaged way. Nonetheless, many of us cringe at any mention of the brains, livers, kidneys, hearts, and tongues my great-grandmother used to cook when I was little. Waste nothing, except the parts that gross us out, seems to be our sentiment. And my vegetarian friends are not exempt: do they realize that fish emulsion, and bone, and blood meal are among the most common and useful organic plant fertilizers? On this planet, life requires other lives.

The meat farmer for the community-supported agriculture program I belong to likes to email us long letters about how many offspring her animals have had and how adorable they look cavorting outside. At one of the weekly farm-share distributions I overheard a member say, "The meat is delicious, but I wish she wouldn't send those emails about the animals skipping around on the farm. It's kind of macabre." I couldn't help wondering just what this person thought free range meant, and if she'd rather the animal had not had such a pleasant existence before it was killed for her dinner.

UPDATE: I stand by everything I originally wrote here, with the exception of the fact that it is now over fifty years, not forty, during which I've been eating meat without having ever killed an animal for food. I'm still not proud of that.

It is no longer normal for us to say grace before a meal. If one of my friends, or more likely their parents, does ask, "Who will say a blessing?" there is often an awkward pause. At our dinner parties these days there are atheists seated beside Christians next to Jews across the table from Muslims and goddess-loving Pagans. Such are the joys of big city diversity. How, then, to say grace on behalf of every individual sharing the meal? And why bother?

I bother because I feel better when I acknowledge where my food comes from and how extraordinary the cycle of life and death is on this planet. I say grace because I am happier believing all life matters. When it is awkward to say it aloud, then I think grace. Maybe I do this because of that lamb I befriended and then ate four decades ago. This is what I say, and I say it directly to the food on my plate:

The energy you give me, I turn into the actions of an honorable life. You will have no cause to be ashamed of being part of my bones. May your spirit travel in joy.

Lamb Mousakka
Serves 12 (recipe can be halved)

The Lamb Moussaka recipe that follows is slow food. There are many steps, many ingredients, and it is so, so worth it. In Greece, moussaka is a special occasion dish, and the time you put into making it is appreciated as a sign of how much you care for your guests. It isn't hard to make though, just time consuming. If you're really pressed for time keep in mind that Step One can be done two days ahead, the whole thing assembled a day ahead, and then just baked on the day your guests are coming. Even people who don't usually like eggplant or lamb like moussaka. It is such a reliable showstopper that one year I made it for six different parties including my Grandma Nea's 95th birthday. Dried eggplant, rehydrated, can be used if you are making it in winter.

Step One (can be done up to 2 days ahead)

2 large onions, finely chopped
2 tablespoons olive oil
1 tablespoon butter
1 cup finely chopped mushrooms
1 pound ground lamb
One 15-ounce can diced or ground tomatoes
3 tablespoons tomato paste
    (or dried tomatoes rehydrated and pureed)
¾ cup dry red wine
½ cup finely chopped fresh Italian flat leaf parsley
1 teaspoon ground cinnamon or spicebush berry
1 tablespoon minced garlic
1 tablespoon dried oregano
1 teaspoon honey

1. Sauté the onions in the oil over medium heat until soft and starting to color, 10 to 20 minutes, stirring often. Add the garlic and stir for one minute. Stir in the tomatoes, tomato paste, parsley, honey, cinnamon, oregano and wine and reduce heat to low. Cook uncovered 30 to 45 minutes until most of the liquid is absorbed or evaporated.

2. Meanwhile, in a separate pan from the tomato sauce, sauté the mushrooms over medium-low heat in the butter until soft and starting to reabsorb their liquid and get fragrant. Remove mushrooms from pan and set aside. In the same pan brown the lamb over high heat. Remove from heat and combine mushrooms and lamb.

3. Add meat and mushroom mixture to tomato mixture. Let cool completely before proceeding with recipe (or store in refrigerator for up to 2 days).

Step Two: The Eggplant

3 pounds eggplant (smaller is much better as far as texture and taste, but use your common sense — don't choose eggplant so small that it takes you an eternity to slice)

Olive oil
Salt
1 cup all-purpose flour

1. Cut off ends of eggplants and slice vertically into 1/4-inch slices. Sprinkle with salt and let sit 30 minutes.

2. Rinse the eggplant under cold water. Squeeze gently in a kitchen towel or between paper towels. Dredge in the flour. Shake off excess. Sauté in a single layer at a time in olive oil over medium high heat, turning once, until brown on both sides.

Step Three: The Béchamel Sauce

4 cups milk
½ cup butter
6 tablespoons flour
⅛ teaspoon ground nutmeg or spicebush berry
¼ teaspoon white pepper
4 eggs, beaten
2 cups ricotta cheese

1. Heat milk in a saucepan just until small bubbles appear along the sides. Set aside.

2. Melt the butter in a pot over low heat until just foamy. Gradually add the flour, whisking constantly for 3 to 4 minutes. Don't let it brown.

3. Slowly whisk in the warm milk until thick and smooth. Remove from heat. Add nutmeg and pepper.

4. Gently fold in the ricotta. Stir in the beaten eggs.

Step Four: Assemble and Bake

2 cups grated Kefalotyri or Parmesan cheese
1 cup dry bread crumbs

1. Preheat oven to 300°F.

2. Lightly grease a 16x10" baking pan that is 3 inches deep, or equivalent. Sprinkle the bottom lightly with breadcrumbs.

3. Place a layer of eggplant in the pan, following with a layer of the tomato-meat mixture. Sprinkle with breadcrumbs and cheese. Repeat layers until ingredients are used up. Pour béchamel-ricotta sauce over the top and sprinkle with any remaining breadcrumbs. Bake at 300°F for approximately 1 hour, until a golden crust has formed on top.

4. Remove from heat and let stand undisturbed 20 to 30 minutes before serving.

🌿 *The Gypsy Summer* 🌿

"No, Lambroula, they are really, truly gypsies," I said to my cousin and childhood best friend.

I was visiting my grandfather in a tiny village in Greece. Almost nine years old, I had rank over Lambroula's not-quite-eight-year-old status. And there really was a community of gypsies camped at the outskirts of my grandfather's village in Greece that summer.

Of course, I was sternly told not to go anywhere near them. And of course, it was impossible to resist.

We ran pretty wild that summer, with little adult supervision. So long as we were home before dark, no one kept track of us. Or maybe they did and I just wasn't aware of that gentle surveillance. In my memory we had hours of unscheduled, unfettered time with the rocky beaches to one side, and the thyme-scented mountains on the other.

The gypsies had set up camp just outside of the village; not so far that we couldn't easily walk there, but far enough that no one would have heard us call if we got into trouble.

The gypsies weren't welcome in town, not even in the small store that doubled as a café. We didn't dare let them see us. And anyway, it was more exciting to sneak our way there, crawling like soldiers on our bellies until we could peer through the tall weeds at their camp.

The gypsy girl was gorgeous, surrounded by women braiding her black hair and painting her eyes. Lambroula and I had snuck up to the camp over an hour before, and it was almost time for our sundown curfew.

It was also, apparently, the start of a wedding at the gypsy camp.

The bride turned and looked directly at us. I can still see her gleaming gaze, the crimson and gold in her dress, the women fussing around her. I knew she had seen us, and I was afraid she would give us away. And then, for just an instant, her eyes met mine directly. She smiled and looked away.

We ran home, grateful to have gotten away with our escapade. But all the while I was thinking about how the gypsy girl had smiled right at me.

For the rest of that summer, I played at being a gypsy bride, calling any road my home, and smiling graciously at the local kids whenever they spied on me.

Me and puppy around the time of The Gypsy Summer

❧ *Sidewalk Bouquet* ❧

By the time I was 6, my mother had remarried and we lived in a Victorian flat across the street from the dance studio she ran with my new dad. We had moved into the flat before she met him, along with two dogs, two birds, a pet white rat, a goldfish, uncounted cats, and a changing roster of human roommates. We inherited this home, and the dance school, from a choreographer Mom had danced for. There were purple floors, blue ceilings with painted stars, a frightening cockroach population, and a party souvenir in the form of graffiti on the bathroom wall behind the toilet that read "On the way back, peanut butter is good." My parents' generation may remember the 1960s and early 1970s as a time of cultural revolution, but I remember wondering when all the grown-ups were going to grow up.

On weekends I was sent to visit my grandmother, who had also remarried and was living in suburbia. It was another world. She bought me black patent leather shoes to wear with nice dresses, and we watched television with dinner (my parents didn't own a TV then). I think that is when I learned my front-of-the-bus/back-of-the-bus skills, or how to shift from rowdy all-night debates about craft with my dancer friends to putting on a gown and having quiet conversations with board members at opening night galas.

All of the hippie décor and the constantly shifting inhabitants disappeared once my dad settled in. The human roommates moved out first, the pets dwindled to just one cat, then none. I helped repaint and wallpaper the walls in subdued colors. We started wearing clothes all the time even at home (which had not been a requirement before), and a new rule required me to wear shoes when I went outside.

I had already been taking dance classes and performing for 3 years when my parents added a children's program to their school, San Francisco Dance Theater. I went from public school to dance class but in between I came and went pretty much as I pleased. I had my own set of keys and could let myself in at home after school. In that pre-soccer mom era, childhood still included great swathes of go-out-and-play time, and in between school and dance I'd call my best friend, Cybelle. "Meet me downstairs in five!" I'd say, and off we'd go.

Cybelle was a daredevil and a tomboy and not remotely interested in ballet. I was a bookworm who spent school recess at the library rather than playing ball. What we had in common was our own sets of keys, liberal parents employed in the arts, and two small neighborhood parks within five blocks of each other. Those two patches of green weren't as grand and wild as Golden Gate Park had been when I lived with Yia-Yia Lopi, but they had good climbing trees and plenty of hidden trails.

At the library, I devoured *My Side of the Mountain*, by Jean Craighead George, in which a young boy not only gets to live off the land solo, but does so with full parental permission (the ultimate kid's fantasy!). I read Laura Ingalls Wilder's *Little House* books over and over, paying special attention to actual recipes and how-to's. I was also an avid reader of *National Geographic* magazine. When I was 11 an issue featured forager Euell Gibbons on a beach feeding a crew of cameramen with the wild edible plants and seafood he had gathered. I was fascinated. I checked all of his books out of the library, along with a few field guides. Two of the plants I read about were the same as those I'd collected with Yia-Yia: dandelion and mustard greens. I fantasized about running away to the woods and being entirely self-sufficient.

I heard my parents' friends talk about people they knew who had *gone back to the land* and reconnected to *Nature* in mysterious ways that had to do with *finding themselves*. It was San Francisco in the '70s. There was no shortage of support for my interest in self-sufficiency skills.

I invented games around my survivalist fantasies. These usually involved sending Cybelle off to do some daredevil stunt that I never would have attempted, and then meeting her back at whichever tree was headquarters for that day. Sometimes these games had homesteading themes. One weekend I decided that it was imperative we collect enough dandelion buds to feed four. I had read that these buds, sautéed in butter, were a special treat. The older buds on long stalks were too bitter. What we wanted was the hard-to-find prize of immature buds still tightly closed and buried at the base of the leaves. Optimistically, I had already invited my parents to lunch that afternoon.

We were way too early in the year for the main flush of dandelion flowers. One thing I hadn't learned yet was that experienced foragers don't waste time hunting for plants that are out of season. At 11, I had taught myself to correctly identify dozens of wild plants, but hadn't yet built up the crucial foraging skill of good timing.

It took hours and both neighborhood parks to provide a small handful of dandelion buds. As Cybelle and I headed back home, I was secretly embarrassed by our measly handful of dandelion buds. But since it had been my idea and I didn't want to seem stupid, I pretended that the scant quantity just proved the ingredient's rarity and worth.

To hear my dad tell it now, he was convinced that I was going to poison them. My mom apparently had more faith in my ability to read a field guide. It is to their credit that they didn't snicker as our handful of flower buds shrank in the melting butter. Finally I divided two spoonfuls into four portions. They were actually pretty tasty.

Recently I walked home from the subway station and spotted some dandelions blooming in a crack in the sidewalk. Every year the timing of the season is slightly different. Many leafy greens become bitter once the plants flower, including such familiar crops as lettuce. I'd thought I still had a week or two in which to get around to my dandelion harvest, but apparently not. I rushed home to collect some of the leaves in my own garden. Who cared if I was tired from a stupidly long workday? I would never forgive myself if I let an entire spring slip by without tasting *horta*. The first mess of wild greens still heralds spring for me just as it did for Yia-Yia Lopi.

I took a colander from the kitchen and headed out back into the garden I share with two guys in the apartment next to mine. A more experienced forager in my forties than I was at 11, I bee-lined for the partially shaded corners where I knew the dandelions wouldn't have flowered yet. There was barely enough light left to harvest by, but my fingers found the tiny round bumps of immature flower buds hidden in the leaves. I added them to my colander along with enough greens to cook down into a side dish for dinner. To celebrate the season, I popped the cork of a bottle of dandelion wine. I didn't feel celebratory, though. I felt restless and edgy within the confines of my one-bedroom apartment.

My cell phone rang. I listened to my friend Julie say that she, too, was having an attack of spring fever. "I still dream of running away to the woods and living off the land," I told her, "but the truth is that I've lived most of my life in small apartments in big cities." There was a pause and then she said, "Leda, honey, you do live off the land!"

We signed off and I served myself the garlicky wild greens. As I tasted my first forkful washed down with another sip of dandelion wine I thought that just maybe she was right about me.

Reintroducing Yourself to a Dandelion

The dandelion, a.k.a. *Taraxacum officinale*, is one of the few wild plants that even die-hard urbanites can usually identify. What kid hasn't blown on a fluffy dandelion seed-head? Nowadays you can buy dandelion greens at farmers markets and upscale gourmet shops, but for those of you who want to forage your own, here are a few tips: There are a few plants such as chicory with similar leaves, but fortunately they are edible, too. Dandelion leaves grow in a rosette, which means that all of the leaves emerge from a central point on the ground. The leaves have sharply and irregularly toothed margins (the name dandelion comes from the French dents de lion, or "teeth of the lion.") The points of the "teeth" face straight out or back towards the leaf base, which is not true of the lookalikes. The familiar bright yellow flowers emerge from the center of the plant, shooting up on leafless stalks. The mature plant exudes a milky sap believed to be useful for treating warts. The slender taproot of this European import is brown on the outside and grayish-white on the inside. Besides eating the leaves and flower buds, you can use the flower petals in fritters or make them into wine. The root can be roasted and ground for a delicious, non-caffeinated coffee substitute (chop the fresh roots fine before roasting in a 300°F oven until they are as dark as you like your coffee beans. Grind in a coffee grinder and brew as you would coffee). All parts of the dandelion plant are medicinal and provide a useful tonic for the digestive system and the liver. Dandelion is also an effective diuretic, one of the few that does not deplete the body of potassium. Another French name for dandelion, pissenlit (to wet the bed), refers to this use. The plant is at its most valuable as medicine just when it becomes too bitter to be palatable. That bitterness comes from the presence of medicinally active alkaloids. If I had to pick just one plant to harvest for both food and medicine it would be dandelion.

Dandelion Wine
Makes approximately 3½ bottles of wine

Dandelion wine is fermented sunshine. —*Jack Keller*

> 2 quarts dandelion flowers, measured before trimming off most of
> the green calyx and all of the stems (you should have about one
> quart once you're done trimming)
> ¾ pound chopped golden raisins
> 1½ pounds honey
> 3 lemons, juice and zest (not the bitter white inner peel)
> 3 oranges, juice and zest (ditto)
> 1 teaspoon yeast nutrient or 2 tablespoons corn meal
> 4 quarts filtered water
> 1 packet wine yeast (available through homebrewing supply
> companies or online. See the Useful Resources appendix.)

1. Snip off most of the green calyxes of the flowers. It's okay if a little
   of the green goes in, but too much is bitter. Put the trimmed petals
   in a non-reactive vessel (no aluminum or iron). Bring the water to a
   boil and pour over the flower petals. After 2 hours, strain and reserve
   liquid, press and discard petals.

2. Bring the strained liquid to a boil. Stir in citrus juice and honey,
   stirring to dissolve the honey. Add the lemon and orange zest and the
   chopped raisins. Remove from the heat and set aside to cool. When
   room temperature, stir in yeast nutrient or cornmeal and wine yeast.
   Cover and leave at room temperature. Stir 3 times daily for 10 to 14
   days.

3. Strain into a sanitized 1-gallon jug and seal with either an airlock
   (check those online homebrewing supply stores again) or a balloon
   with a single pinprick in it to allow gasses to escape but keep
   detrimental bacteria out. After 3 weeks, siphon or carefully pour
   the liquid into another sanitized jug, If there are more than 2 inches
   between the top of the wine and the neck of the bottle, top off with a
   syrup of equal parts honey and water.

4. When wine is clear rather than cloudy, wait 30 days then siphon or carefully pour it into another jug, top up if necessary, and refit airlock or balloon. Repeat this procedure every 3 months for 9 months until almost no sediment is forming on the bottom of the jug any more.

5. Pour through a funnel into bottles, cork (get a hand-corker from that homebrewing supply company. It is cheap and really worth it. You don't want corks popping prematurely, do you?), and age for another year before drinking. Patience. This is bottled sunshine. Served chilled and toast the return of spring.

*Dandelion (*Taraxacum officinale*)*

❧ *Blackberry Hill* ❧

We sat on the floor in Studio Two in a semi-circle around our teacher, Jody White, and read aloud from our journals. My parents had hired Jody to direct the children's program at San Francisco Dance Theater. Jody decided that the heart of the program, just as important as ballet technique class, would be Theater Arts, a weekly catch-all class in which we learned to think like artists. She brought in her husband, Ralph, to teach acting classes, as well as lighting designers, mimes, dance historians, physical therapists, and costume designers. We formed a junior company called Chrysalis. Though we performed some ballet oldies like the peasant pas de deux from *Giselle* and the 19th-century *Pas de Quatre*, we also wrote and choreographed our own shows and published collections of our theater arts class writings.

I got excited about being an artist in that class. Before then the studio and the theater had just been my second home, a place where mom worked and I hung out, taking class but just as often running out the door to head to the park. But in Jody's theater classes I learned that the arts mattered, that artists mattered, that everything I had ever seen or thought or felt could be transformed through the alchemy of creativity into something beautiful, or thought-provoking, or moving, or disturbing, something that would directly affect other people. I also learned that I didn't have to limit myself to just one art form. Instead of that leaky old warning about jacks-of-all-trades being masters of none, Jody encouraged us to be multi-faceted. Her reasons were pragmatic: she wanted our vocations to pay the rent someday. Three or four marketable skills meant that if one job didn't pan out there would be alternative work in the theater, without having to wait tables in between jobs.

By the time these ideas were motivating me to take several dance classes a day, Cybelle and her mother had moved away and I no longer had a buddy interested in foraging in the park. All of my best friends were at the dance school or at American Conservatory Theater where I had a full scholarship as an acting student. I lost interest in regular school, where I had been at the top of the honor's roll. When September loomed I tried to hold on to summer's freedom, cutting school to go to the library. Then, with a stack of books in my backpack and hours until my first dance class, I headed to Blackberry Hill.

Blackberry Hill was a corner property that had been vacant for so long the volunteer shrubs had grown taller than I was, and a thicket of thorny blackberry canes created a tangled screen that hid the street. The remnants of a front garden were hidden among the weeds. Trailing rosemary, daylilies, and unkempt roses were tucked in among opportunists such as wild oats, mouse-eared chickweed, and dandelion. Aside from the orange butterflies and white cabbage moths that shared it with me, Blackberry Hill was my private haven. The rest of the world faded while I was there, even the street traffic sounded distant. I disappeared into my books or wrote in my theater arts journal, eating blackberries instead of the school lunch I had missed.

One day I arrived at Blackberry Hill and found freshly bulldozed soil, no plants, a chainlink fence, and a construction sign. It looked much smaller than it had when I was nestled with a book among the wild oats.

I went to the ballet studio early that day. I watched the midday classes and helped the scholarship student working the front desk fold fliers for a mailing. There was no one to tell about Blackberry Hill, no one who'd known about it except me. None of my ballet friends would care about an overgrown lot. Telling my parents would mean confessing how much school I'd been missing. So I folded fliers and remembered the cabbage moths landing on the blackberry canes, and I didn't cry. I felt quite fierce and loyal actually. I imagined myself becoming Defender of the Green, finding every wild nook and cranny of the city and rescuing those green spaces from annihilation. But mostly I thought that now I had nowhere to go during the day except school or the dance studio.

Many years later, when I was dancing with Jennifer Muller's company, she choreographed a work called *The Spotted Owl*. It was a multi-media piece with both live and recorded dialog. Marty Beller and two other musicians played live, and the cues were complicated. Sometimes Marty would use a sight cue from our dance steps to start the next musical section, sometimes a line of dialogue; sometimes our dancing was timed to his drums, sometimes to the recorded words. Those recordings included a list of endangered species, "red wolf, fewer than three hundred," and so on. The whole piece was about endangerment—of wild species but also of human freedom and creativity. Jennifer wrote the closing curtain monologue for me. This was something special, as dear to my heart as any dance solo would have been. The words were a riff on the alphabetical memory game, Grandmother's Trunk. In the traditional road-trip game you start out saying "In my grandmother's trunk I would put an apple," or something else starting with A. Then the next game player says, "In my grandmother's trunk I would put an apple and a bottle," or something else starting with B. And the game continues like that, each person adding something alphabetically but also having to remember everything the other players added before them.

In *The Spotted Owl*, Grandmother's Trunk was an end-of-the-world speech about what my character would save if she only had this one chance. It included things like the future, habitats, manatees, and zinnias. The first thing on the list, for the letter A, was an artist. The final line was "I am an American artist." I performed that monologue for several years, and each time I began it I thought of Blackberry Hill before it was bulldozed. *In my grandmother's trunk, I would put...*

With Michael Jahoda in Jennifer Muller's The Spotted Owl, *1995 Photo by Tom Caravaglia*

UPDATE: Jody White and her husband Ralph both passed away a few years after this was written. Before she died, Jody and I were working together on a couple of projects, including a series of illustrations she drew in response to this book (in addition to being a brilliant dance teacher, Jody was a talented visual artist).

BLACKBERRY TIPS

Berries freeze well, but if you put a bunch of blackberries into a plastic freezer bag or container what you'll get is a big block of blackberry ice. Instead, put the berries in a single layer on a plate or cookie sheet and freeze. Once frozen they can be put into a freezer container but will remain loose so that you can take out only what you need. This method also works with vegetables that do not need to be blanched before freezing and that you only need small amounts of from time to time. Chopped bell peppers and onions are especially useful prepared this way.

Blackberry leaves, and the leaves of other members of the Rubus *genus including raspberries, can be dried to make tea. Although they have none of the caffeine of tea (*Camellia sinensis*), Rubus leaves do contain tannins that create a similar mouth feel. They don't have a lot of flavor on their own though, so I combine them with other herbs. Here is one of my favorite blends:*

Everyday Tea

(Based on a blend originally invented by friend and forager Melana Hiatt)

Equal parts dried raspberry or blackberry leaves, mint, red clover blossoms, and nettles. Put ½ cup of the mixture in a pint jar and pour boiling water over. Cover and steep 20 minutes. Strain and enjoy with or without honey.

Blackberry Jam
Makes 1 to 2 half pint jars. Recipe can be doubled.

1 quart fresh or frozen blackberries
¾ cup honey
Juice of 1 lemon

1. Stir the berries and the honey together. Cover and let sit at room temperature for 30 minutes.

2. Add the lemon juice and bring to a boil in a non-reactive pot over medium-high heat. Cook, stirring constantly, until the mixture is just slightly runnier than you want your finished jam (it will thicken a little bit as it cools). Ladle into half-pint canning jars that you have sterilized in boiling water for 15 minutes. Leave half an inch of head space. Screw on two-piece canning lids. Process in a boiling water bath* for 5 minutes. Remove jars from water and let cool completely before moving the jars (moving the jars while they are still warm can cause the canning lids to lose their seal).

For boiling water bath processing instructions, see page 105.

Part Two: Kitchens on the Road

❈ Small Trees, Big Oranges ❈

By the time I turned 14 I was fully committed to becoming a professional dancer. I'd already been training and performing for 8 years by then, but I'd been just as interested in running away to the woods someday as in following my mother's path in ballet. But after my best friend Cybelle moved away and Blackberry Hill became an apartment complex, I didn't spend much time outdoors or at home anymore. Dance became my home. At 15, I announced that I wanted to move to New York to pursue my career. My parents said I was too young. At 16, I got a full scholarship to American Ballet Theater's school and moved to New York. I signed my first company contract a week after my 17th birthday.

My life as a full-time professional dancer wasn't nearly as straightforward as it might sound. Not because of the hard work and low pay. Having grown up around dancers, I was expecting that. But try as I might to contain my life within city limits, I kept finding myself on the wilder side. Even during moments that should have been elegant I often felt like the knobby-kneed kid with tangled hair running barefoot in the park.

I remember one fancy dinner in a lovely home on Manhattan's Upper East Side. As I reached for a glass of champagne, the sleeve of my black chiffon dress slid back revealing vivid red scratches. "What happened to your arm?" asked prima ballerina Cynthia Gregory, seated to my right. Where to begin? I thought.

Orange trees have thorns. I'd just spent a month picking oranges in the eastern Peloponnese for 3.5 drachmas a kilo. My boyfriend was still there trying to come up with enough money to get home, or at least out of Nafplion.

I'd ended up there because I'd gotten into the habit of continuing to travel after the end of each dance company tour. I loved touring and wanted to extend each trip as long as I could. I was never in a hurry to go back to the States. I would change the date of my return ticket and keep going until I ran out of money or was due back in New York for rehearsals. Sometimes I got so low on funds that I couldn't afford to hold out until my rescheduled return flight. Too proud to borrow money but stranded in a foreign country without working papers, often I had to invent work. One of my improvised jobs was dancing on the streets of Avignon while two very nice British boys ran the music boom box and collected coins from the crowd for me. Another time I played panpipes in front of a shop in Bern, Switzerland until the owner chased me away (very politely, too, giving me a map of which streets busking was permitted on). In Florence, I cut up a pair of bronze silk pants that had been part of my dressy reception clothes on tour. I sewed the fabric into little purses and tried to sell them on the Ponte Vecchio. I only sold one purse all day and regretted having hacked up a nice pair of pants.

This way of surviving and supporting my travel habit didn't seem odd to me. I had a role model: when I was 5 and in Greece with my mom, Papou wouldn't pay for us to go back to the States. So Mom talked her way into a dance job on a ship in exchange for our passage. I learned to trust that I could always improvise a solution to getting home.

I ended up picking fruit off thorny orange trees after a tour that ended in Genoa. Half of the company was going back to New York, the other half splitting up for separate travels. I kept my hotel room for one extra night after the others had left. That night the local TV news ran a spot on our last performance of the tour. I watched myself on the screen flying through the choreography that up until yesterday had been my reason for being on the road. Now I was alone with no per diem and no real plans as to where I'd go next.

Meanwhile my boyfriend, a dancer from San Francisco, had gotten a job with a small modern-dance group in Jerusalem. They needed a female dancer, so I headed to Israel to join him. Jerusalem was fascinating and many of the people there were warm and generous, but I was instantly miserable. The caliber of this particular company was not as high as the one I'd been touring with, and several of the dancers had bad tempers. There were often arguments during rehearsals. There were fleas in the apartment the company found for us. But what really made me decide to leave were two events signaling that I was changing in ways I didn't like: When I first arrived, I wasn't comfortable with the guns off-duty soldiers carried, but by my last month I was so used to them that when the nose of a machine gun repeatedly bumped my thigh on the bus one day I shoved it aside with annoyance but no fear. It disturbed me that

I was so calm about it. That same week I was shopping in the *souk*, the local market. The *souk* was always crowded and boisterous with lots of shoving. When someone pushed me away from behind to grab at a tomato I'd been reaching for, I jabbed my elbow in their direction without thinking about it. When I turned around, I saw that I had just hit an old woman. I was turning into someone I didn't like and I was painfully homesick. I asked for a meeting with the director the next day and announced that I was leaving before the end of my contract.

My boyfriend and I hadn't been paid for all of the weeks that we had already danced there, so we didn't have enough money to fly back to the States. We booked third-class passage on a boat out of Israel, stopping on Rhodes and ultimately landing in Greece.

We went to see my great-aunt in Paralia Sergoulas first, but she didn't have the money to help us get home. I pulled out my trusty copy of *Work Your Way Around the World*. According to that backpacker's bible, it was the right time of year to pick up some under-the-table money working the citrus crop in Nafplion. All we had to do was find a place called Harry's Bar and show up there around 6 a.m.

Nafplion is a postcard-pretty town with a Venetian fortress in the harbor and a Turkish citadel above steep twisting streets. We rented a room for 2000 drachmas a night and celebrated the progress of our adventure with a bottle of retsina.

The next morning, Harry's was packed. We elbowed our way in for a cup of coffee alongside would-be migrant workers from France, Australia and Ireland. We heard a rumor that the farmers were only hiring existing teams who were proven workers, and so we gratefully accepted a French couple's invitation to join their team.

The way it worked was that when a truck pulled up everyone ran outside waving to get attention and shouting that they had the best workers, the fastest team. The farmer pointed to those he wanted and they jumped into the back of his truck. Everyone else went back inside to wait for the next farmer to drive up.

If you were chosen, you haggled. The ideal was a day rate. We heard some people had gotten 3500 drachmas a day when the season started, but now we'd be lucky to get 2800. Most farmers wanted to pay by weight, offering so many drachmas per kilo of oranges. Those farmers always promised that they had easy-to-pick "small trees with big oranges, ie. light work and easy money. Usually we'd get to the grove to find out that not only were the trees tall with small oranges (discouraging when you're being paid per kilo of picked fruit), but the gypsies had already stripped the lower branches of the easy-to-reach fruit.

The gypsies worked for cheap, only 1500 drachmas a day. They finished early by "cheating the field." We were supposed to work each tree as a team, some standing on the ground picking the easy to reach fruit, some on ladders, and one, called The Monkey, who climbed up the tree and got the oranges on the very top. I was usually The Monkey. By 10 a.m. we'd already been picking for a few hours. Sometimes a hand from below would thrust a bottle of Metaxa up to where I was perched in the tree. I'd take a breakfast swig to stay warm and go back to picking.

We were not supposed to move on to the next tree until the one before was completely picked. The gypsies would zip through a grove ignoring ladders and grabbing only the fruit in easy reach, leaving the harder to reach oranges for us. I have always been attracted to gypsy music and culture, but in Nafplion I cursed when I climbed out of the truck and saw a field they had "cheated."

Besides day rate vs. kilo rate, one of the things we negotiated for was a hot lunch. When you have been picking oranges from dawn until noon, fingers frozen but not daring to slow down because you are being paid per kilo, a hot lunch is the difference between hating life and reminding yourself that you love being a traveler. When the farmer's wife showed up with a steaming pot of chicken stew with vegetables, that was heaven.

It was impossible to save any money. Even one rainy day without work was enough to dig a hole in our savings. To keep myself sane I needed to believe that I was still a professional dancer, so a few times a week my boyfriend joined me in doing a ballet barre holding onto an old stone wall in a field.

Some of our money was spent at Harry's drinking beer and playing cards. The other players were a motley collection of characters. Some of them hadn't had a fixed address for years. They could get rough. Once the cops came checking passports because a transient had gone missing and murder was suspected.

Those co-workers made me nervous, but others I despised as too soft. I was one of the travelers working because I actually needed the money, not one of those who worked because they wanted "an authentic experience of another culture." It was The Tourists vs. The Travelers. I had reason to disdain The Tourists: the weight of the oranges we picked was totaled at the end of each day and the pay distributed equally among all members of the team. Even one slow worker meant lower wages for the rest of us. I could barely manage a polite smile for the pair of American girls who told me that I really needed to relax and appreciate how beautiful the frost was on the oranges in the dawn light. The gypsies laughed at us for being suckers, we derided the tourists as dilettantes, and at the end of the day we were all back at Harry's.

After a few weeks the citrus season was about to end and I still didn't have enough saved for a ticket home. My boyfriend decided to try his luck with the next harvest, olives further west on the Peloponnese. I discovered that pride is as negotiable as a hot lunch, and got on the phone to borrow plane fare. I watched my drachmas dwindle as I tried to get through on the public phones at the post office, calling choreographers I knew back in New York to ask if they had work for me. Francis Patrelle said yes, he did. "Rehearsals start next week and there's a meet-the-artists fundraiser this Friday that you have to be at. By the way, are you in shape? Where have you been dancing since I saw you last?" he asked.

I slept on a friend's couch my first night back in New York. While I was enjoying a long shower I was also letting the steam smooth the wrinkles out of a black chiffon gown that had been stuffed in the bottom of my suitcase since the end of the tour in Genoa. The following night I put on the dress and took the subway to Dances Patrelle's fundraiser.

"Well, Cynthia," I said, setting down the glass of champagne, "you're not going to believe this, but two days ago I was in a town called Nafplion picking oranges…"

UPDATE: When this book was first published I had no idea that within a few years I would be living in Jerusalem again, twenty-five years after the events I'd written about. As I write this annotation, my kitchen is filled with food from the very souk that so disturbed me all those years ago. Life doesn't merely surprise me; it astounds.

Peloponnese Chicken with Orange
Serves 4

This recipe always reminds me of those hot lunches we got to eat in the orange groves on our luckier afternoons. Serve it up with some crusty bread and a salad for a simple but company-worthy meal.

4 boneless, skinless chicken breasts
1 pint jar of home canned tomatoes,
    or one 13.5 ounce can of whole tomatoes
½ teaspoon freshly grated orange zest
¾ cup freshly squeezed orange juice (from about two oranges)
¼ cup dry white wine
2 tablespoons extra-virgin olive oil
4 cloves garlic, peeled and minced
1½ teaspoon dried oregano
Leaves from a 4-inch sprig of fresh rosemary
    (or four 1-inch tips), chopped
1 teaspoon salt
½ teaspoon ground cumin
½ teaspoon ground coriander

1. Combine orange zest, orange juice, wine, half of the garlic, 1 tablespoon of the olive oil, salt, oregano, cumin, coriander, and rosemary. Place chicken in a shallow dish or bowl. Pour marinade over chicken and let marinate for 1 to 2 hours.

2. Sauté remaining garlic in olive oil over low heat in a large skillet for 30 seconds, stirring. Add the tomatoes with their juices and raise heat to medium-high. Cook for 5 minutes, stirring occasionally and using your spoon to break up large tomato pieces into smaller chunks.

3. Place chicken breasts in pan and cover with half of the marinade. Cook for 6 minutes over medium high heat. Turn and cook an additional 6 minutes on the other side.

4. If sauce is still too thin, raise heat to high and boil rapidly for a couple of minutes to evaporate excess liquid.

5. Serve each chicken breast with some of the sauce spooned over the top.

Peloponnese Chicken with Orange

🌾 *The Sea Takes It Away* 🌾

It had been 20 years since my mom and I traveled to Greece when I was 4. We expected changes. My great-aunt Zoitsa had an electric stove now, she wrote in a letter, and running water—she didn't need to go out to the old pump anymore. The mailman came twice instead of once a week, and on a motorcycle rather than a donkey. Costas and his brothers had opened a small discotheque that ran for six weeks during the summer, frequented by the occasional tourist but more often by cousins who had moved to the city but still came back to the village for holidays.

We knew there would be changes, but as the bus followed the curvy road from Athens and we saw the rocky Greek countryside we got excited for the things we remembered. Surely the water would still be as clear as ever, so clear that the oval stones and dark sea urchins at bottom were visible even from the pier. Surely the culinary trinity of olive oil, lemon, and garlic was eternal, as were the salty goat cheeses and the heaped platters of *psariki*, the fried fish too small to sell. Electric stove or no, Thea Zoitsa would still be taking round brown loaves of bread out of her wood fire oven. The plastic tub of kalamata olives, made according to my grandfather's recipe, would still sit below the white cabinets displaying John F. Kennedy ashtrays he'd brought back to Greece after 40 years in the States.

Thea Zoitsa greeted us with a "special just for you" platter of what looked like slices of Wonder Bread. She had taken the ferry to Agios to buy this pre-sliced loaf, sure that it would please our American palates. She was so proud of offering "what you are used to." Oh no, we said, you didn't have to. We love your bread, the brown bread from the old oven. Really. No, no, we were told. That was poor people's bread. Did we think they were still peasants? She could afford white bread now.

She said she did still use the old wood fire oven for special party dishes such as moussaka because they just didn't taste right when made in the electric. But for day-to-day living, what a relief not to have to gather all that fuel and mind the fire and clean out all that ash.

We had been looking forward to the sourdough tang and chewy density of her brown bread. She was grateful for the respite from the relentless physical labor she'd known all her life. Everyone lost out, because even Thea Zoitsa couldn't pretend that the pre-sliced, plastic-wrapped bread from the store was good to eat.

When I traveled, I kept encountering this clash between the deliciousness of the old ways and the convenience of modern store-bought food. I listened to people reminisce about what wonderful cooks their grandmothers had been, only to follow up by saying thank god we don't have to work that hard any more and anyway who has the time?

Once I rented a house in Southwest France with my dad and my husband. There were wonderful old chestnut trees growing on the property. When I complimented them to a local he told me that it was only in recent years anybody ate the nuts. How could that be? I asked him. I loved chestnuts. In my family, there is a *yemisee*, a Greek rice stuffing, that is turned into a special holiday food by adding boiled chestnuts. He explained that during World War II chestnuts were what people turned to when wheat was scarce. Labor-intensive to prepare, and lacking the gluten that enables wheat dough to rise, ground chestnuts came to be thought of as a famine flour rather than a flavorful treat.

On another trip, several people in Ireland assured me that the blackberries in their hedgerows were inedible. This was a blatant lie—I enjoyed them as a trail snack when I went for a walk every morning. Eventually one old-timer admitted that yes, you could eat them. "My sister used to make a decent jam with them, but that was because there wasn't anything else during the war. Made tea from the leaves, too, when the regular ran out. Got everything from the field those years."

My Greek aunt didn't want to eat her magnificent brown bread because she associated it with being poor and a peasant. My French and Irish friends turned their backs on rich chestnuts and perfectly ripe blackberries because of a war that ended over 60 years ago. Still, they had options. They knew how to fire up the wood oven if they wanted to, how to make that brown bread, how to leach the bitter tannins out of the chestnuts and dry and grind them for flour, how to make that hedgerow jam. Most people I know don't know how to do any of those things. They don't have to because they are surrounded by food for sale from all over the globe. But the abundant variety offered by the shops and restaurants still limits their choices to what strangers provide. If there was an actual war on our home turf, if the trucks couldn't get through and the stores ran out of food, how many of us would be able to live off the landscape the way the my French and Irish friends did in World War II? It is not so much a question of whether or not they wanted to as that they could. In just two generations we have lost that option.

Back in the village, my mom and I sat sipping our tiny cups of thick coffee, *skehto* (black) for me, and *metrio* (medium-sweet) for her. We had lost the brown bread battle, but were enjoying the summer afternoon and the sound of small waves lapping at the pier my grandfather had built. Thea Zoitsa came out of the house looking like a postcard Greek yia-yia: thick stockings, black kerchief tied under her chin, slightly stooped, carrying a bundle of something towards the pier. When she got there, I was horrified to see her throw a plastic bag of trash into the clear sea. "What are you doing?" I exclaimed. She looked baffled by my outrage. "This is what we have always done," she said. "Don't worry. The sea takes it away."

That night, writing in my journal, I wondered what it was like to have lived in an era when people still believed that there was someplace "away" where the tide could take your trash without consequence. She probably looked at me and wondered what it was like to have lived a life that had never seen war firsthand, someplace where the electricity always worked and the stores never ran out of bread. We were both naive in terrible ways.

There are two bread recipes below. One is as close as I've been able to get to Thea Zoitsa's brown bread. She died years ago without passing on her recipe. And even if I had the recipe, I don't have her wood oven. So the recipe that follows is not her bread, but it is very, very good bread that comes close to capturing the experience of that bread we ate on my first trip to Greece. The only leavening in it is sourdough starter because that is what people used before the days of packaged dry yeast. It is a good bet that Zoitsa must have been using sourdough to get her bread to rise. In this recipe, the sourdough not only leavens the bread but also provides the tangy flavor I remember in hers. Instructions for getting a sourdough starter going and maintaining it follow the recipe. Sourdough bread takes a long time to make but most of that time is rising time while you are sleeping or away at work.

The second recipe is my solution to wanting homemade bread but being short on time. It is a buttermilk soda bread. The buttermilk gives it some of the tang that sourdough bread has, although the texture is different. You can mix the ingredients and have it in the oven in less time than it takes to run to the store.

Sourdough Brown Bread
Makes 1 large loaf

1¾ cups active sourdough starter (see below)
2 to 3 cups whole wheat bread flour (bread flour is higher in gluten than regular flour. If you can't get it, use a mixture of half all-purpose and half whole wheat flours)
¼ cup milk
1 teaspoon olive oil
1 teaspoon honey
1 teaspoon salt

1. Stir together 1 cup of the sourdough starter, honey, oil, milk and 1 cup of the flour. Cover and place in the refrigerator overnight.

2. Add another ¾ cup of starter and the salt. Work in additional flour in one-third-cup increments, kneading by hand or using the dough-

hook attachment of a mixer. Make sure each addition of flour is fully incorporated into the dough before adding more. Do not add too much flour — the dough should come cleanly away from the sides of the bowl but still be fairly soft. Different flours absorb different amounts of liquid (I so wish I was looking over your shoulder to tell you when you've added enough!). Err on the side of too little rather than too much.

3. As soon as all flour is incorporated, let the dough rest for 20 minutes.

4. Knead for 10 minutes either by hand or with a dough hook in a stand mixer. Lightly coat a large bowl with oil. Place the ball of kneaded dough in bowl and turn to coat all sides with oil. Cover with a damp towel or plastic lid and let rise 5 to 8 hours (i.e., while you're at work) until doubled in size.

5. Press down the dough and let rest 10 minutes. Shape the dough into a round loaf. Sprinkle a baking sheet with cornmeal and place the loaf on it. Cover with a damp kitchen towel and let rise until almost doubled in size. How long this will take depends on how active your sourdough starter is. Mine takes about 2 hours for the second rise. If you have to run out the door before your dough has finished rising just put it in the refrigerator. The cold will slow down the sourdough yeast without killing it and you can pick up where you left off when you get home.

6. Slash the top of the loaf about half an inch deep with a sharp knife or razor. This will allow moisture to escape during the baking and prevent the loaf from cracking on the sides. Place in a cold oven. Do not preheat. Turn oven on to 350°F. The bread will be done in 30 to 40 minutes when the top is golden and the sides start to pull in away from the loaf pan. Or (my preferred method), when a digital thermometer inserted into the center registers 205°F.

7. While still hot from the oven, take the bread out of the loaf pan, brush it with melted butter or olive oil, and wrap in a clean, dry dishtowel. This yields a tender crust. If you prefer a crunchy crust, skip wrapping it in the dishtowel. Cool on a rack for at least 15 minutes before diving in.

MAKING A SOURDOUGH STARTER

A sourdough starter is just yeast, flour and water. The yeasts are alive and are what make your bread rise. There are many different ways to get a starter going, but here is a recipe that has never failed me:

> **1 cup organic grapes, fresh or frozen, ideally unwashed (all grapes have wild yeast on their skins, which is what historically has made them the perfect fruit for winemaking)**
> **1 cup filtered water (do not use unfiltered tap water because the chlorine can kill the yeast)**
> **1 cup flour**

1. Mash the grapes in a bowl. Whisk together with the flour and water. Cover and leave at room temperature for 3 days, stirring at least once a day (more is better).

2. Strain out the grapes. Feed your starter another ½ cup of flour and ½ cup of filtered water. Your starter should be frothy at this point from lively yeast action. Scoop it into a glass quart jar. Cover and store in the refrigerator.

MAINTAINING YOUR STARTER

1. Once a week, take your starter out of the refrigerator and spoon it into a bowl. Stir in 1 cup of flour and 1 cup of water. Cover and leave at room temperature for a few hours or overnight. Your starter is now "refreshed" and active and ready to use to make bread or other recipes (sourdough pancakes — yum! See page 114). Once you've taken out what you need for your recipe, give your starter another ½ cup each of flour and water before returning it the refrigerator.

2. If you are going to be unable to refresh your starter for longer than a week, put it in the freezer.

Buttermilk Soda Bread
Makes 1 round loaf

Preheat the oven to 375°F.
Grease a baking sheet or line it with parchment paper or a silpat mat.

1⅔ cups whole-wheat pastry flour (pastry flour makes this bread more tender. If you can't get whole-wheat pastry flour, use a mix of half all-purpose and half whole-wheat flours)
1 teaspoon baking powder
½ teaspoon baking soda
½ teaspoon salt
2 teaspoons caraway or anise seeds (optional)
1 egg
⅔ cup buttermilk
¼ cup melted butter,
    plus 1 more tablespoon reserved for brushing on finished loaf
1 tablespoon honey

1. Whisk the dry ingredients together in a large bowl.

2. In a separate bowl, whisk together the wet ingredients.

3. Pour the liquid ingredients into the dry ones. Stir to incorporate the flour. Don't stir too much though — it's okay if there is still a little dry flour here and there, and for this dough, lumpy is good. You want the dough to still be somewhat soft and sticky, but coherent enough that you can shape it into a loaf. If the dough seems too goopy, add more flour a little at a time. I sometimes need to add as much as another third cup of additional flour. Some cracks on top are okay and actually make the finished loaf more attractive in a rustic way.

4. Scrape the dough out onto your baking sheet. Shape it into a disk approximately 5 to 6 inches in diameter. Bake 25 to 35 minutes until golden. While still hot, brush with remaining tablespoon of butter. Let cool on a rack.

❉ *A Turkey on the Roof* ❉

I didn't learn how to cook from the women in my family or from my dad, though they were all extraordinary cooks. I watched and I ate, but I was never asked to help in the kitchen and, to be honest, I wasn't all that interested. I learned to cook because I needed to make my per diem last on tour. It was rarely enough to cover eating at restaurants every night. In New York, there were delis and coffee shops and other cheap options. But you can blow through a dancer's income pretty fast if you're eating out in Paris or Tokyo.

Tour was too often a contrast between the opportunity to dance and travel against the scary possibility that I wouldn't be able to cover the bills when I got home. So I developed certain habits that will be familiar to any dancer reading this. If the hotel breakfast was a buffet, you can bet I slipped some extra containers of yogurt, along with cheese, a roll, or a banana into my bag for lunch.

Dinner was the priciest meal, so I tried not to eat it out too often. I did sometimes, of course. Part of the fun of touring was getting to taste the local cuisine. But I just couldn't afford it every night.

There was one great tour when I got to spend 5 weeks in Paris with Jennifer Muller/The Works. I had my own room because there were an odd number of people in the company that year and I got the single room. I bought a heating coil, a plastic cutting board, a small aluminum pot, and a mug. With my Swiss army knife, plus a fork and spoon pilfered from the hotel restaurant, I had a kitchen. There was no refrigerator in my room, not even a mini-bar, but it was November and cold outside. I put my perishable groceries in plastic bags, tied those to the shutters, and hung them out the window. I made some filling one-pot meals in that room, pastas and soups mostly, all washed down with that season's newly released (and cheap) Beaujolais Nouveau.

I was teaching by then, company class for Jennifer Muller/The Works, but also freelance. One job gave me the chance to spend a month or two each year in Switzerland teaching and choreographing at a school called Dance Loft. My first home-cooked meals there didn't consist of much more than what I'd learned to do for myself on tour: I'd open a can of tomatoes, another can of green beans or corn, and serve that to myself on pasta with lots of pre-grated packaged cheese. But with every visit my meals got more interesting.

In Switzerland, I discovered the farmers' market in St. Gallen and looked forward to going there on my days off. The food on sale in March was so totally different from what I saw when I arrived to teach in September. The produce seduced me with its freshness and vivid colors. Sometimes they even had dandelion greens, which made me think of foraging in the park with Yia-Yia Lopi.

Soon I developed a kitchen routine that I fell into each time I arrived. I had a short shopping list of kitchen essentials, and it is still my basic list when I move into a kitchen on the road: olive oil, salt, garlic, vinegar or lemons, dried chili peppers, honey or sugar, and some basic herbs like oregano — the same spices my Greek relatives used every day.

Each time I got back to New York, Diet Cokes and bagels from the deli seemed less tasty than they used to. I started to set up my kitchen at home the way I did on the road and sought out the farmers' markets (only a handful then) in the city.

When you have great ingredients you have to learn what to do with them. By the time I had been back to Dance Loft six or seven times I'd become a decent if not an exceptional cook. One year I was there for the whole month of November. The school provided me with a lovely little apartment that I shared with the directors' son, Boris. The directors, Rut and Roland, were friends as well as colleagues, and when I realized that I would be there for Thanksgiving, I casually invited them over for dinner. They were intrigued by this American holiday and asked if I would prepare the traditional dishes they had heard about. Of course, I said, not realizing what I was getting myself into.

I don't remember who the students were that year or what I taught them, but I do remember every detail of that meal. Preparations for it began 3 weeks before the actual event. Although I had originally envisioned cooking for four or five of us, Rut and Roland kept calling to let me know that another guest was curious to experience "a real American Thanksgiving." Eventually it became clear that I would be cooking Thanksgiving dinner in Switzerland for 12.

There was no whole turkey large enough for 12 people to be found in St. Gallen. Why should there be? There is no equivalent Swiss holiday in November, and who eats a whole turkey except during the holidays? Not to mention that it is an indigenous American bird. Ultimately, we had to order one from Zurich. Other Thanksgiving essentials, including cranberries, pumpkin, and sweet potatoes, also proved hard to find. "A potato that is orange inside and sweet?" repeated Roland skeptically.

Two days before the dinner I still had not found any pumpkin, canned or fresh, nor any other winter squash suitable for a pie. One day I spotted two pumpkins in a seasonal decorative display in a florist's window. I asked the proprietor how much they cost. She wouldn't sell me just the pumpkins. I'm not sure she even understood that I just wanted the pumpkins. I bought the whole display. (It is much easier to find pumpkins outside of North America now than it was then, as well as sweet potatoes and even the rare can of cranberry sauce.)

Another cultural difference that hampered my Thanksgiving feast preparations was space. I was working in a classic northern European kitchen with a waist-high refrigerator instead of the behemoth that occupies a corner of most American kitchens. It included a freezer that boasted less than a square foot of space. When Max, as I named the turkey, arrived from Zurich, he obviously wouldn't fit in the diminutive freezer. I stored Max on the roof, grateful that the weather outside was freezing.

Even once all the ingredients were assembled my cooking adventure wasn't over. The oven dial had "gas mark" numbers rather than Fahrenheit temperatures, the salt seemed oddly saltier than I was used to, and I swear the sweet potatoes took longer to cook than they did when I made them in New York.

On the day of the dinner, it was fascinating to see that what was so familiar to me was exotic to my Swiss friends. "Do we exchange gifts? Sing special songs?" they asked. No, I explained, you mostly just eat. I decided not to get into the dubious history of the Pilgrims and the Indians, though I did explain that most of the ingredients were truly native to the Americas. I also decided not to mention anything about the tradition of television football (vs. soccer, which to them is football). The guests found all of it amusing but strange. They also thought that pumpkin pie was a completely weird idea. "A pie made from a squash?" one of them exclaimed, halting a forkful halfway to her mouth when she found out what it was. To them, winter squash, including pumpkin, was for savory dishes like soups, not dessert.

Since that Thanksgiving in Switzerland, I have cooked for people wherever I have stayed for more than a few days. I've cooked on campfires, and I've cooked on a restaurant-caliber stove in the kitchen of a mansion. Along the way I've become a good cook, and I've enjoyed sharing my meals with friends all over the world.

Some of my best memories are of those kitchens on the road. I remember the sound of a fire popping in the outdoor kitchen of a rented house in France, and I have a photo of my dad taken minutes before we ate that dinner: he is grinning over a huge coil of sausage we were about to throw on the grill. I remember the 80 year-old Frenchman who arrived from next door with a bottle of wine tucked under his arm, a little uncertain what to expect from these tourists who had invited him to dinner. I remember another kitchen with doors and windows open to the tropical night. A Brazilian thunderstorm lashed the palm trees and a small group of us cooked by candlelight because the power had gone out. The caramel sweet aroma of an improvised coconut milk rice pudding bubbled up from a pot on the stove. And I remember feeling, at least on those nights, that I was home.

Coconut Rice Pudding
Serves 6

---

2 cups cooked rice
1½ cup (one 13.5-ounce can) coconut milk
¼ to ¾ cup water
¼ to ½ cups dulce de leche (see note)
1 banana
One 1-inch strip of lemon peel, yellow part only
    (use a vegetable peeler)
½ teaspoon ground cinnamon
½ cup grated coconut

1. Combine the rice, coconut milk, lemon peel, ¼ cup of the dulce de leche, and ¼ cup of the water in a pot. Bring to a boil. Reduce heat and simmer, uncovered and stirring often, for 20 minutes. Add more water if needed to prevent sticking.

2. Peel banana and cut in half lengthwise. Cut each half again lengthwise so that the banana is quartered. Cut crosswise into ½-inch chunks.

3. Remove lemon peel from pudding and add the banana chunks. Continue to stir the pudding as it simmers until the rice has absorbed most of the coconut milk. It should be thick and creamy, but not soupy. This will take another 5-10 minutes.

4. Turn off heat. Stir in the cinnamon. Taste and add more dulce de leche if you want it sweeter. Serve warm, sprinkled with the grated coconut.

Note: Dulce de leche is available canned in most supermarkets. If you can't find it, you can substitute condensed milk. But dulce de leche has a caramel flavor that condensed milk does not, so it's worth the search.

WINTER SQUASH, INCLUDING PUMPKIN, AND WHAT TO DO ABOUT IT

Hopefully you won't have to buy your pumpkins from a florist's display as I did! By the way, pumpkin is a winter squash, and all of them can be prepared in similar ways.

Storing Winter Squash

You can store winter squash, including pumpkin, acorn, delicata, carnival, hubbard, and others, at room temperature for at least two months if there are no soft or blemished spots. To store for an additional month or two, wipe the rind down with a paper towel and a little vegetable oil. This prevents molds from attacking your squash.

Winter Squash Puree for Soup or Pie

1. Cut your winter squash in half. Scoop out the seeds and stringy pulp (a serrated grapefruit spoon works well for this). Save the seeds for the recipe on page 58. Preheat an oven to 400°F. Place the squash cut side down in a baking dish. Add half an inch of water to the baking dish. Bake 30 minutes to 1 hour until the flesh is soft and the rind is starting to brown in spots.

2. You can eat the squash as is, with a little butter, a scrape of nutmeg, and a bit of brown sugar, maple syrup, or honey in the cavity. Serve with a spoon. Or you can turn your baked squash halves into a puree that can be frozen and used for soups or pies:

3. Scoop out the flesh of your baked squash. Compost the peel. Either mash the flesh with a potato masher or blend until smooth in a food processor. The winter squash puree can be stored in freezer bags or containers for up to 6 months. It is still safe after that, but the quality will start to degrade. Use your puree in winter soups and Thanksgiving pies.

Maple and Cider Vinegar Glazed Winter Squash
Serves 1 to 20, depending on how many squash you use.

The recipe below is a fall or winter treat that is best served at room temperature and can be made a day ahead. Piled high on a plate and served as finger food, it turns very simple seasonal ingredients into a party appetizer or side dish worthy of a feast

> Winter squash, such as acorn or butternut
> Olive oil (or duck fat is sublime)
> Cider vinegar
> Maple syrup
> Garlic, peeled and minced, 1 clove per pound of squash
> Salt
> Minced fresh parsley
> Red pepper flakes (optional)

1. Cut the squash in half. Scoop out the seeds and compost them or save to make toasted squash seeds (see recipe below). Cut off the stem and flower ends. Remove the skin with vegetable peeler for small squash such as delicata or carnival. Use a sharp knife to peel thicker-skinned varieties like butternut. Cut into ½-inch thick chunks or crescents.

2. Over medium-high heat, add enough oil or duck fat to coat the bottom of a large frying pan. When it is hot enough that the surface is starting to ripple, add a single layer of the squash. Do not overcrowd the pan — there should be at least half an inch of space between each piece.

3. Cook the squash until the first side is starting to turn brown, about 8 minutes. Turn each piece with tongs and cook until the next side browns. Turn again until all sides are browned.

4. Sprinkle the squash with garlic, a splash of vinegar, a drizzle of maple syrup, and a pinch of red pepper flakes if using. Stir constantly for 1 minute. Remove the squash to a plate and sprinkle with the minced parsley and salt.

5. Add more oil to the pan if needed and start your next batch of squash. Proceed as above until all the squash has been cooked. Serve at room temperature.

TOASTED PUMPKIN OR OTHER WINTER SQUASH SEEDS

This works best with seeds no bigger than half inch in length, such as delicata or butternut seeds. With small seeds, there is no need to hull them before toasting.

1. After you've scooped the squash seeds out of the squash, separate them from the stringy pulp. Note: this is easier to do with mature squash or those that have been in storage for a month or two; i.e., the ones you get in January and February.

2. Spread the seeds on a baking sheet. They will have more flavor if you leave them unwashed with the pulp juice clinging to them. Let dry at room temperature at least 1 hour or as long as overnight.

3. Place in a 250°F oven for 20 to 30 minutes, stirring occasionally. I use my toaster oven for small batches. If after this initial toasting they are not yet turning golden brown, increase the oven temperature to 300°F and toast for a few minutes more. Keep an eye on them as they can go from done to burnt quickly during the last few minutes of cooking. They should be crunchy, with no chewiness in the hulls, but no darker than golden brown.

4. You can eat them as is, or toss them with vegetable oil and salt, or with soy sauce, and put them back in the oven for a few minutes (or until dry if using soy sauce). These are wonderful as a snack, or sprinkled on salads.

❧ *Mint Tea and a Ride Not Taken* ❧

Back when I arrived in New York at 16 to finish my dance training, I was all about ambition and diets. Forget about wild edible plants. I needed a different set of survival skills to survive my new environment. I turned my back on what suddenly seemed a childish interest in the natural world and began a conflicted relationship with what my dance teachers called "my instrument."

One day in variations class one of my ballet teachers mentioned that I was getting some curves. I didn't menstruate again for a year after that because I starved myself. No mere dieting for me, oh no, I had to dabble in anorexia. I was 5 feet 5 inches tall and by the end of my first summer at ABT I weighed in at ninety-three pounds. It was in that condition that I auditioned for, and got, a contract with ABT's second company. Gone were the dreams of running away to live off the land in the wilderness. They'd been replaced by an obsession with getting my leg extension 6 inches higher and whether or not I'd be overdoing it if I had lowfat instead of nonfat yogurt for lunch.

I shared an apartment with a New York City Ballet dancer and two other girls from ABT. I remember what was in our refrigerator because our menus and our shopping lists never varied: iceberg lettuce, diet salad dressing, grapefruits, apples, hard-boiled eggs, non-fat milk, diet soda, and Baco-bits. In the cabinet was All-Bran cereal, popcorn, cinnamon, Pam cooking spray, salt and pepper, coffee, and Sweet-n-Low. Sometimes for a treat we'd spray a frying pan with Pam, slice apples, and fry them sprinkled with cinnamon, a dieter's version of apple pie. The smell was wonderful, almost as if we really were about to eat a slice of warm-from-the-oven, home-baked apple pie.

It was an exciting decade to be a young dancer. I saw the movie *The Turning Point* at least a dozen times, echoing the way my mom's generation had adored *The Red Shoes*. *The Turning Point* was shot in the exact same ABT studios where I was training. It was the height of the dance boom, and dancers I shared studios with were featured on the covers of *Time Magazine* and *Newsweek*. Baryshnikov rehearsed in the studio next to where I took class. This is heady stuff when you are 16. And hey, it was The Seventies. My school counselor blessed my decision to drop out and leave home with the statement, "Send me tickets to one

63

of your shows someday." (To my shame, I never did and I don't remember her name). My dad told me recently that he, at least, expected me to come running home within 6 months. As I write this, it has been 35 years. I might have turned my back on my childhood love of nature forever but for a wild night in Slovenia 10 years later.

I was on tour with a very good pick up company, Manhattan Ballet. The past 2 days had been magical. The night before I'd danced one of those rare performances in which everything goes right, and the summer festival audience in Ljubljana responded by giving me multiple curtain calls. The next day I had off, and by early morning I was on the back of my lover's rented motorbike, one arm around his waist and mist blowing vigorously from the hills into my hair. We paused at a sign pointing to Dragonia and laughed as if it had been put there just for us. We had found a place named after dragons, of course we had. We met a potter who invited us her into her home. Her eyes were naturally violet, her face wrinkled with age but her voice sultry. A young man related to her (I forget how) showed up with a wild boar he had just killed draped over his shoulders. That boar became our dinner. More of the potter's family members and their friends showed up. One of them was a balloonist named Luca Skywalker. As a Star Wars fan, I loved that.

After the meal, we bid farewell to the potter and followed some of her family to a house where they were staying. At least I think they were all staying there. Very little English was spoken and much wine was swallowed, so I am a bit fuzzy on the details. We communicated in a mix of broken English, Serbo-Croatian and pantomime. An oversized full moon rose, lighting the hilly landscape and the old stones of the building we were in. I was in love, looking forward to dancing a leading role the next night, and in a gorgeous place having an adventure with new friends. This, I thought, is how life is supposed to be.

Someone handed me a cup of steaming water and passed a bowl filled with sprigs of fresh mint. I held the cup and my handful of fragrant stems and leaves and for a moment I was confused. "I think you're supposed to put it in the water," my lover whispered in an amused and condescending tone. He was married, older, my mentor as much as my boyfriend. His opinion mattered too much to me. I was hugely embarrassed that I didn't realize the mint leaves were meant for the cup of hot water. The kid I used to be, the one who foraged for wild edible plants in San Francisco's parks and sold her homemade herbal salves instead of lemonade at the corner stand, she would have known what to do with that bunch of mint. I ducked down towards my cup, inhaling the sharply aromatic steam and thought, what happened to me?

We were invited to go on a midnight horse ride. I didn't know how to ride a horse, but I did not want to admit that. I wanted to be the kind of woman who would know how to jump up on a horse and ride off under a full moon. I made up some lame, complicated excuse for why I was going to stay back at the house. My lover took off with several of the others in a rush of hoof clatter. I washed dishes with a couple of women who had also stayed behind. Then I paced the courtyard, peevishly wishing my lover had been sensitive enough to turn down the ride and stay with me. Especially because his wife was joining our tour tomorrow, and so surely these last few hours together should be his priority?

But there were three uncomfortable truths caught in my throat as I waited for his return: 1. I really, really wished I could have gone on that ride. I hated it that a mundane limitation such as not actually knowing how to ride a horse prevented me from participating in an adventure that wouldn't come my way again. I was used to telling life what I wanted to do next, not to being shown where I couldn't go. I hated this. 2. He was married, and worse, I'd met his wife and really liked her. Tomorrow he would be with her instead of me. Shit. 3. That mint tea. How could I have missed something so obvious as dropping the damned mint leaves into the hot water?

Since I couldn't retroactively go on that horseback ride or delete the fact that I'd had an affair with a married man, I focused on the one thing I could do something about, which was reclaiming my passion for plants and nature. As usual, I overdid it. Within a year I was selling herbal sports medicine products to my fellow dancers. Within 10 years I applied for and got a tuition grant from Career Transition for Dancers and went back to school part time. I got a certification in Ethnobotany from The New York Botanical Garden and started teaching there and at The Brooklyn Botanic Garden. I got a lot of mileage out of that cup of mint tea.

I still don't know how to ride a horse.

UPDATE: Shortly after this book was published, Ricky (the man I wrote about in this chapter) found me online. This time, neither one of us was married.

He read the book, which he enjoyed except that he accused me of taking artistic license with the moon. I described it here as being full, but he assures me that there was no moon that night. He vividly remembers the darkness itself as one of the most extraordinary elements of that horse ride he took without me.

When I wrote this chapter, it had been almost twenty years since we'd seen each other, and I had no thought in my mind that I would ever see him again. I was mistaken. We've been together for over six delightful years as of this writing.

During those years I've lived with him on two continents, gotten my first driver's license (at age 50), written four more books, learned how to do a headstand, and studied another language.

*But I **still** don't know how to ride a horse.*

*Taking a nap on Ricky's shoulder
after a whale-watching trip that was part of our honeymoon*

Mint Jelly to go with Wild Boar
(or other Pork, or Root Vegetables)

My hands-down favorite homemade jelly, foolproof and delicious. Great with pork, lamb, poultry, or yes, wild boar, but also grain and root-vegetable-based vegetarian dishes. I make at least two batches of this every year because it makes a lovely gift.

3 pounds apples, chopped
  (apple cores and peels saved in the freezer work fine)
8 cups water
Sugar
Lemon juice
4 to 6 fresh mint sprigs, tied together at the stem ends

1. Wash fruit and add water. Put into a covered saucepan. Place over medium heat and boil for 30 minutes, stirring frequently. Drain through a jelly bag. Do not squeeze the bag or you will have cloudy jelly — this draining step can take as long as overnight. This should make about 3½ cups of juice.

2. In a large, non-reactive pot, add 1 tablespoon of lemon juice and ¾ cup of sugar per cup of apple juice. Bring to a boil, stirring often. The bubbles will go from being small and foamy to large and climbing the sides of the pot. At first if you lift a spoonful of the jelly up in a large spoon and pour it back into the pot the last drop off the spoon will be a single drop. Eventually, the last bit poured off the spoon will separate into two distinct drops. When the jelly reaches the "2-drop" stage, add the herbs. (When the last of a spoonful of jelly sheets off the spoon rather than remaining in two drops, it is done even though it will still look completely liquid.) Turn off the heat immediately. Remove herb bundle. Ladle into sterilized jars, seal, and process in a boiling water bath for 5 minutes*. Allow to cool undisturbed for 8 hours.

*ABOUT STERILIZING JARS AND THAT BOILING WATER BATH

To sterilize jars, completely cover them with water. Bring to a boil and boil 15 minutes. Turn off the heat and leave in the hot water until ready to fill with jelly.

For instructions on how to process the jars in a boiling water bath, see page 105.

Apple jelly with mint, served on oat drop biscuits

With Anton Wilson in Jennifer Muller's Broken Wing, *1996*
photo by Tom Caravaglia

Part Three: Grounded

Cronewort, a.k.a. Mugwort (Artemisia vulgaris)

🌿 *Cronewort Moon* 🌿

My first date with my future third husband was brunch on Manhattan's Upper West Side. James told me later that he was incredibly nervous and showed up an hour too early. To pass the hour, he bought a copy of *The New York Times*. He had trouble focusing on the newspaper, but did notice that the science section had an article on something to do with herbs. Knowing of my interest in plants and herbal medicine, he saved it for me. When we sat with our popovers and coffee an hour later, he tried to ease an awkward pause in the conversation by handing me the article. "Well! That's to the point," I thought when I saw the title, "Herbs for Birth Control May Be Effective." I looked up to see him blushing. Turns out he that he had been too distracted earlier to actually register what the article was about.

I heard James before I saw him when I showed up for the first day of rehearsal for a new ballet Francis Patrelle was choreographing. There were singers in the ballet as well as dancers, and I heard a luscious baritone voice belting out the final note of Sondheim's *Foxtrot* as I walked into the studio. I saw a lanky young man with sky-blue eyes and thought, "He's good. Should be fun to work with."

I once commented to my friend John that the men in my life had been all over the map as far as type. Ten years older, my age, over a decade younger, tall, short, blue-eyed, brown-eyed — I didn't seem to have one particular type that I was attracted to. John, who's met more than a few of my men, said, "Oh honey, you so have a type! Every one of them has had a dreamy bedroom voice."

So there was James, with his dreamy bedroom voice, and he shared my passions for theater, nature, and travel. We tried to be professional and not give in to our attraction, and we almost succeeded. But on closing night I realized that I might never see him again, and that was just unacceptable. The curtain came down and everybody was hugging and congratulating each other and I ran across the stage and literally jumped into his arms. He looked surprised but happy and spun me around and wouldn't put me down for a long time. I knew it was probably a terrible idea (several friends told me so), and that I should have known better. Hearts were certain to get broken. I invited him to brunch. It seemed like a safer invitation than dinner, with enough wiggle room for me to back out with a "just friends" option.

And there we sat at brunch, James blushing while I tried to come up with something to say after reading that headline, "Herbs For Birth Control May Be Effective."

He asked me to teach him about plants and what different herbs were for. When I suggested that he start with one or two plants and really learn to identify them, learn what their uses were, and ideally grow them himself, he asked for books and wanted to memorize the information. I gave him books, but learning about plants that way is about as dry as unbuttered toast. A field guide or herbal can describe a plant, but it is not same as touching and smelling and tasting the plant itself.

The first plant he identified in the field with me was burdock (*Arctium lappa*). He made me laugh by saying the name over and over again in a deep, gruff, character voice that suited the rough, foot-long leaves: "Burdock." I laughed every time he said it. Burdock's prickly seed-heads, the burs for which the plant is named, got stuck on our clothes as we bent over the plants. I told him about how the person who invented Velcro was supposedly inspired by burdock. James kept an eye out for park rangers while I dug up a few of the long straight roots. He told me my digging technique was inefficient and went on and on about leverage until finally I handed him my digging stick and told him to have at. His method didn't work any better than mine, and I laughed at him. Burdock roots are notoriously difficult to unearth. They are worth it though, both as a vegetable and a medicine. "Burdock gets to the root of the problem," I told him, a description that helps me remember that burdock is good for deeply rooted chronic complaints, especially skin and digestive problems.

That night we ate the slivered roots in a stir-fry. The Japanese call burdock *gobo* and it is a favorite ingredient in their cuisine. It shows up for sale at Asian markets and sometimes at farmers markets. We only ate half of that day's harvest because I wanted to tincture the rest to use medicinally. I put the chopped-up roots in a glass jar and he poured vodka over them. "That," I said, "is how you make an herbal tincture. In 6 weeks or so, it will be ready to strain and put in little dropper bottles like the ones you can buy at the health food store." After finding the plant, digging it up, tincturing it, and eating it for dinner, James knew burdock.

Burdock is a weed, one of those plants that thrives where no human planted it and does just as well in the city as in the country. Maybe better. Weeds like the disturbed soil we humans are always creating. Once James had learned to identify burdock he saw it everywhere. I love it when that happens to me after I've learned to identify a plant. It's as if I've been introduced and can no longer just walk by as if I were ignoring a stranger. I know what it looks like. I know its name. It isn't "just a weed" to me anymore.

The next plant James learned was cronewort, *Artemisia vulgaris*. A more common name for this aromatic herb is mugwort because in past centuries it was used in Europe as a flavoring for mugs of beer, the way hops are today. It is even more ubiquitous in the city than burdock, and like burdock it has both edible and medicinal properties. I love to crush the leaves, green on top and silver-white on their undersides, and inhale their wild, spicy scent. Cronewort as food is more of a seasoning than a vegetable. I've seen *Artemisia*-flavored soba noodles for sale in health food stores. James and I didn't eat it much, but we burned it and bathed in it and wove it into wreaths.

I sometimes went to get acupuncture treatments for minor dance injuries. The acupuncturist, a tiny woman in a fifth-floor walk up in Chinatown, burned clumps of dried cronewort, which she called moxa, on the tops of her acupuncture needles. It was bizarre to look down and see dozens of needles sticking out of my legs, each emitting a thread of smoke as if my leg was on fire. But the actual sensation was soothing, and I could feel the warmth unclenching my muscles. At home, (we were living together by then), James and I skipped the needles and experimented with an alternate method used in China: place very thin slices of fresh ginger on sore muscles and then burn a little wad of dried cronewort on top of the ginger. Sounds strange, but it feels wonderful.

One year James helped me make little dream pillows for Christmas gifts, using the same pattern I'd made up when I sewed my cut up silk pants into purses to sell in Florence. Along with cronewort, I stuffed the pillows with dried rose petals, lavender, and cloves. I found the recipe in a reprint of a 17th-century herbal, one of those wonderful old books with a colorful illustration of each herb alongside a description of its uses. The herbal said that sleeping near a pillow stuffed with cronewort leaves would cause vivid recall of dreams. One person we gave a dream pillow to called to ask me what the hell I'd put in those sachets because she'd had unbelievably horrid nightmares. I said that I didn't think the herbs could be held responsible for the content of her dreams, only the remembering of them. But just in case I have never made dream pillows since then.

Artemisia vulgaris was one of the plants in that *New York Times* article on herbal birth control James gave me on our first date. Actually, it doesn't prevent conception. What it does do is jumpstart menstruation that is late due to stress, travel, or changes in diet. It opens other kinds of flow, too, and not just in women.

Cronewort gets its genus name, *Artemisia*, from the moon goddess Artemis. I think of her when there is a half moon in the sky looking like Artemis's drawn bow. I remember a night with a half moon when I came home from an especially long rehearsal day. I asked James to make a cronewort infusion to add to my bath, knowing it would unravel my tense muscles and make me break into a cleansing sweat. The half moon was bright in the small bathroom window that night. I climbed into the bath even before the infusion was ready, grateful for the steaming water. James came in and added the Artemisia infusion to the bathwater. Then he added himself. After that, James knew cronewort.

When James learned that in Sicily it is believed that cronewort gathered at the summer solstice and hung in wreaths protects the home he suggested we follow that tradition. For the rest of our years together, each summer we burned the wreaths from the previous year, placed our newly made ones on our heads, and gave each other a kiss for luck in the year ahead. Then we hung the new wreaths over our apartment's front and back doors.

When he left me abruptly one November day 11 years after that brunch with the *New York Times* article, I smashed his cronewort wreath into a bag of his stuff that I had packed for him because I couldn't stand being surrounded by so many reminders. The next year on the solstice, I left a message on his voice mail asking him to burn the wreath. I burned mine and didn't make another for years. I told this story to my teacher, herbalist Susun Weed. I said I was never going to make another wreath because it was just a superstition: it hadn't protected my home, at least not the home I shared with James. She scolded me, replying, "Life is change. You say cronewort creates change and flow, then you blame it for not 'protecting' you by equating protection with no change. Unfair! Please make another wreath."

There is a cronewort wreath hanging over my door again.

Artemisia vulgaris is a take-over artist, the quintessential weed, popping up in cracks in the sidewalk and in empty lots between buildings. I wonder if James thinks of me when he sees it. It grows everywhere in New York City.

With Jonathan Riseling in Francis Patrelle's Macbeth, *1995*
photo by Eduardo Patino

Dancer's Bath

4 parts dried cronewort (*Artemisia vulgaris*)
2 parts dried comfrey leaf (*Symphytum officinale*)
2 parts dried chamomile flowers
   (*Matricaria retucita* or *Anthemis nobilis*)
1 part dried rosemary (*Rosmarinus officinalis*)
1 part dried ginger root (*Zingiber officinale*)

1. Put ½ cup of the combined herb mixture in a 6-inch square of cheesecloth or a 3x5 inch muslin bag. Tie closed, but not too tightly. You want the water to be able to penetrate to the center of the herb bundle easily.

2. Bring 1 quart of water to a boil. Pour over the herb bundle in a non-reactive heat-proof container such as a quart canning jar. Pour the boiling water over the herb bundle. Cover and let steep for half an hour.

3. Fill bathtub with comfortably hot water. Pour the infusion and the herb bundle into the bath. Squeeze the herb bundle to extract as much liquid as possible. Get in and soak for at least 15 minutes. You can rub the herb bundle directly on especially sore muscles. Expect to keep sweating for a while after you get out of your bath.

ABOUT THOSE PLANT NAMES

Plants have two kinds of names, common and scientific. The scientific name is made up of two words loosely based on Latin, e.g., *Artemisia vulgaris*. The first word, always capitalized, is the plant's genus. The second, never capitalized, is the species. The scientific binomial isn't there to confuse you. It's there to make sure everyone knows exactly which plant you are talking about (even if you are talking about it to people from another country). There is only one scientific binomial for each plant everywhere in the world. But there are many common names for each plant (mugwort, cronewort) and every language has its own common names for plants, which can get confusing.

Burdock (Gobo) Stir Fry

½ **pound burdock root**
¼ **pound carrots**
1 **tablespoon soy sauce**
2 **teaspoons honey**
2 **tablespoons mirin**
1 **tablespoon white wine**
1 **tablespoon sesame seeds**
1 **tablespoon vegetable oil**

1. Peel the burdock root and julienne it into matchstick-sized strips. The peeling is optional. If you do peel the roots, you will have a milder dish. For a strong, mushroom-like flavor, wash but don't peel.

2. Soak the burdock matchsticks in water for 30 minutes.

3. While the burdock is soaking, peel the carrot and julienne it into matchsticks as you did with the burdock root.

4. Toast the sesame seeds in a dry skillet over medium low heat, shaking the pan often, for a few minutes until fragrant and just starting to color. Do not allow to burn.

5. Mix the soy sauce, honey, mirin, and wine.

6. Drain the burdock in a colander. Spread on a kitchen towel and pat dry.

7. Put the vegetable oil in a frying pan or wok over high heat.

8. Add burdock and fry for 2 minutes, stirring.

9. Add carrots in the hot pan and fry for 2 more minutes, stirring constantly.

10. Stir the soy sauce mixture into the vegetables. Sprinkle with the sesame seeds.

11. Remove from heat and serve immediately.

Burdock Stir Fry

❧ *From the Ground Up* ❧

There was a lavender-colored rose with a spicy scent like cloves in that Brooklyn community garden. It was one of the victims of the developer's bulldozer, but I remembered its unique fragrance for years afterwards. I can't be positive that it is the identical variety, but there is a rose with pale purple petals and that same wonderfully spicy smell leaning from a neighbor's home into the parking lot of the building where I live now. I always feel comforted when I bury my nose in its blossoms.

I lost two gardens in 4 months. The first was the Greene Avenue Community Garden next door to the apartment where James and I had tended a patch of herbs and vegetables for 8 years. The privately owned land had been a community garden for 25 years. Because it was private property, we always knew that we might lose the use of it some day. Hoping for a buffer of time to rescue our most cherished plants, the garden members had negotiated a contract that promised us 30 days notice. We got no notice. One January morning we woke to the sound of bulldozers. We ran outside and saw the upturned ground and I felt gutted. A rosemary shrub that had flourished for me, disregarding every warning that it wouldn't be hardy in our area, was lying on its side, roots exposed. The raspberry patch that on late summer afternoons had been covered with fruit, and beside which we'd buried one of our cats, gone. The big white birch tree with its beautiful curling bark still stood, but it too would be cleared for a new multi-story building that would soon completely shade out the back yards of all the brownstone houses on our block.

After that loss, I spent more hours than I ever had in the tiny garden that came with our one-bedroom basement apartment. I could cross that garden in eight steps. It had just come into it's own. The perennials were well established and in spring it was especially glorious. The woodland ephemerals — red trillium, azure windflower, jack-in-the-pulpit, white bloodroot flowers, violets — were just losing their flowers and the early fragrant roses about to open when I found out that we were being evicted from our apartment. My immediate response was to go into the garden and start digging and bagging the topsoil. I was literally digging up the garden to take it with me. At the time it made perfect sense to me. After all, it had taken 8 years to turn that garden's soil from a compacted, rubble-filled wasteland into fertile loam. That soil represented years of my life, and I couldn't stand to throw it away.

Besides, I told myself, the soil in our next garden would almost certainly need amendments, topsoil and compost at the very least. It would be expensive to buy all that we'd need at a garden center. I was saving us money by digging up our garden, our rich earthworm-populated soil. The truth was that I was crazy to even be thinking about another garden. We had one month to find a place we could afford in New York City. James was unemployed and I was working numerous dance jobs trying to make up the difference. Our friends said forget it, you can't afford a garden apartment, just sign a lease and get a roof over your heads. You can always look for another place later. But I balked at the thought of life without a garden. That garden had been my haven, and I cared about it so much that sometimes I turned down out-of-town jobs if they meant missing a crucial part of the gardening season. In my mind there were only two possibilities: either we were going to leave the city or we were going to find someplace with a garden.

Two weeks before we had to move out we started packing. We still didn't know where we were going to live. I still insisted on a garden. I didn't meet my friends' eyes because I was afraid of seeing the pity mixed in with their compassion, not to mention the confirmation that I'd lost my mind. James told me later that he never expected me to stick with him after that eviction. I'm still surprised he thought that. If I had lost him at the same time I lost my home and two gardens I really would have lost my mind. But I admit that if you had asked me that spring which I loved most, my husband or the garden I was digging up, I might have said the garden.

Possibly the garden rescuing impulse is genetic. At 85 years old my Grandma Nea learned that she was losing the house she'd lived in for decades because her husband had made a mess of their finances. The first thing she did when she found out was transplant her prized roses into a friend's yard and then call to tell me about it. After her husband died, she gardened in an assisted-living apartment even smaller than where I live now. Her balcony was so full of potted plants that there was barely room to step between them, and indoors she began an orchid collection.

I like to think I have a lot in common with Grandma Nea, especially her gardening and cooking skills. Let's not discuss the husbands.

Okay, okay, we'll discuss the husbands. We might as well get it out of the way: In my early 20s I married Paul. I left him because I was young and discontented, but we remained friends until his death in 1995. In his will he left me a suitcase and a black leather motorcycle jacket, which tells you all that you need to know about that marriage. My second husband, Bill, is still a good friend despite the fact that I left him for husband number three, James. James and I were together for 11 years.

Just in time, we found a garden apartment in Park Slope, Brooklyn. When we moved, our entire first U-Haul truckload was garden stuff: plants, the soil I'd dug up from our old garden, tools, a compost bin, organic fertilizers, stakes, pots. My friends Scott and Todd started a new community garden and I signed up for a plot so that between it and the new apartment garden I'd have almost as much land as what I had lost. The first thing I planted in Scott and Todd's garden was a rooted raspberry cane I had rescued from the bulldozers in the Greene Avenue Community Garden.

Many plants survived that emergency change of address, and some of them are in my garden still. One is a clump of garlic chives that has endured more than one transplant to a new address. I first grew it from seed in a container on a West 26th Street rooftop garden. At that time I was married to Bill, a nonsmoking, rarely drinking man. I used to sneak up to the roof for a cigarette and a beer and spend time talking to the neighbor who eventually bequeathed his planter boxes to me. Cigarettes and husbands are long gone from my life, but that garlic chives plant is still with me.

Soon after we moved to our new home in Park Slope, I flew back to San Francisco for my grandmother's 88th birthday. One day while I was there, I walked past an unremarkable apartment building on the corner of Fillmore and Vallejo streets. It was the same corner that Blackberry Hill had graced 25 years earlier. I stood staring at the building, trying to reconcile it with my memories of berry juice and butterflies and skipping school to write in my theater arts journal. A woman opened her window, noticed me, and waved. I returned her wave; it wasn't her fault that once upon a time her building was my favorite hideaway.

As I write this it occurs to me that there is nothing special about having lost so many green havens. It's just my personal equivalent of farmland converted to suburban asphalt, of shiny new streets named after long-uprooted trees. I am just another early 21st-century hybrid who has spent most of her life living in cities while loving the countryside.

The first thing I did when we moved into our new apartment was to set up a compost bin in a back corner of the garden. I salvaged the bin from the community garden on the morning when the bulldozers woke us up. The second thing I did was ask James to clear out the ivy that was covering the ground, and to build three triangular raised beds according to a design I sketched. I spread the topsoil I had dug from our old garden into the beds.

And, because it was still spring, I started planting.

The steps leading from my apartment back door to one of my Brooklyn gardens

Garlic Chives Vinegar
(Also works with other herbs)

When my garlic chives plant blooms each summer I make the flavored vinegar recipe below. This becomes the basis for a lazy salad dressing because the only other seasoning it needs is a little salt. Just use 3 to 4 parts extra-virgin olive oil to 1 part herb vinegar and add salt to taste. Garlic chive plants are often for sale at farmers markets, or you can start yours from seed. See the Useful Resources appendix for some of my favorite plant and seed sources. Or you can use regular chive blossoms, or even just chives (the leaves, which are the part most people are familiar with).

Loosely fill a clean glass jar with garlic chive (*Allium tuberosum*) blossoms, or other fresh herbs. Cover with wine or cider vinegar. After 1 month, strain out the blossoms. The vinegar is now strongly infused with the garlicky flavor and aroma of the garlic chive flowers. This vinegar is terrific in salad dressings and marinades and makes a unique gift.

Apple Scrap Vinegar

The next time you make apple pie or applesauce or anything that uses a lot of apples, save the cores and use them to make this vinegar, which works beautifully for the herb vinegar recipe above.

> **Apple cores**
> **Sugar or honey**
> **Water**

1. Mix 1 tablespoon honey or sugar per cup of non-chlorinated or filtered water. Place apple cores in a ceramic or glass bowl and cover with the sugar-water solution. Cover the bowl with a dishtowel and leave at room temperature for 1 week if made with sugar water, up to 2 weeks if using honey. During this time, stir vigorously at least once a day.

2. When the color of the liquid starts to darken, strain out the fruit.

3. Keep at room temperature, stirring at least once a day, for 2 weeks to 1 month until the liquid smells vinegar-y and tastes sour. Funnel into a glass bottle, cap, and store away from light.

Homemade Wine Vinegar

To make wine vinegar, you need to start with some unpasteurized "live" vinegar. Bragg's cider vinegar is a good brand to use. Besides that, all you need is some wine. One thing to be aware of is that the sulphites that are often added to wine can prevent healthy vinegar bacteria from doing their thing. All wines have some natural sulphites, but the wine industry adds extra to some wines. This is rarely a problem with red wines, but if you want to make white wine vinegar you should start with one that is organic or specifies no added sulphites on the label.

**1 part unpasteurized "raw" vinegar, such as Bragg's cider vinegar
3 parts wine**

1. Combine the vinegar and the wine in a wide-mouth glass or ceramic jar or bowl. Cover with a dishtowel or a paper towel secured with a rubber band.

2. Stir several times a day for the first few days. Vinegar bacteria are oxygen-dependent, and the stirring helps expose more of the wine to air. So does the wide-mouth vessel you have your vinegar-to-be in.

3. A gelatinous disk will form on the surface of the liquid. It looks alien, but don't panic. This is the "mother" of the vinegar and means that the vinegaring process is taking place successfully.

4. At this point you can add a little more wine from time to time. When the vinegar tastes and smells sour enough, it is ready to use. Over time, your vinegar can become unpleasantly strong. Most commercial vinegars are diluted with water for this reason, and you can do the

same. (See note below about vinegar strength for making pickles safely.) When your vinegar is ready, bottle it in a jar with a small neck. At this point you want to exclude as much air as possible to prevent the vinegar from getting any stronger.

5. Once you've made vinegar, always save a little to get the next batch going.

Note: do not use your homemade vinegar to make pickles unless you have tested it to be sure it contains at least 4.5% acetic acid. Most commercial vinegars are between 4.5% and 6% acetic acid (check the label). You need this much acidity to prevent harmful bacteria ruining your pickles. To test your homemade vinegar, order an acid titration kit from any of the many home winemaking supply stores online. See the Useful Resources appendix for web sites you can order acid titration kits from and those with detailed instructions for testing your vinegar.

Homemade vinegar

❧ *Raspberry Cordial* ❧

"I was saving it for something special," my dad says. I scowl at him. I have just discovered that my dad never ate any of the preserves I gave him last year. Every winter I come back to San Francisco for the holidays, and a few weeks before my departure I mail myself a heavy box of homemade preserves I intend to give as gifts. Not only are the preserves I gave him last year untouched, but so are most of the ones from the year before that.

"It's depressing," I say, trying to rein in the edginess in my voice. I know he loves the taste of my raspberry jam, of my sharp and tiny cornichon pickles, of my green tomato chutney and my sage mint jelly. When he visits me in Brooklyn he eats all of them and asks for seconds. But here the jars are coated with dust. The dusty jars seem like evidence of the depression he's complained about recently. His conversation during this visit has dwelled on things that happened years ago, as if there is nothing new in his life worth reporting. I feel that if I could just convince him to open those jars and dig in with a spoon his taste buds would be flooded with flavor, and that would somehow drag him into the present and out of his doldrums. I am not comfortable with how much he is clinging to the past.

"I just won't give you any more," I say, "since you don't like them anyway."

"No, no," he says, "I love them, that's why I was saving them."

I take a deep breath and leave the room. Across the hall from the kitchen is a small room that he uses as a pantry. It is about the size of my entire bedroom 3000 miles away in Brooklyn. The door has a cut out near the bottom for cats that lived here four decades ago. There is an accumulation of recycling waiting to be taken out and a shelving unit. On one of the shelves is a large plastic tub containing several pounds of rancid walnuts. I carry it back to the kitchen and start pouring walnuts into the trash.

"You shouldn't buy so many at a time, and you should always store nuts in the refrigerator or the freezer so they don't go rancid," I say, "And anyway, you live alone, like me. You don't need to buy in bulk."

"Costco only carries things in bulk. That's why everything there is so cheap," he says.

"Is it still cheap when you have to throw out rancid food?" I say, marching back out of the kitchen towards the pantry. My father's choices disturb me.

Behind the empty space where the walnuts had been I find a dusty green bottle with one inch of liquid left in its bottom. A handwritten label dangles from its neck: "From the Garden of Leda & James." I stand staring at that bottle, remembering. I don't need to open it to know that it contains raspberry cordial I made years ago. I know how it will pour, slightly thick yet translucent and ruby bright. I remember my dad visiting us, and the three of us toasting with this homebrew.

"Show him the raspberry patch," James said, and the three of us headed out the back door of our one-bedroom basement apartment, glasses of cordial in hand. We walked across our tiny shade garden, through the gate we'd built into our back fence, and into the Greene Avenue Community Garden next door where the raspberries grew.

I don't need to open the bottle to remember any of that, but I do. I open the bottle and breathe in a cautious whiff. It should be vinegar, it should be the worst dregs of fermentation after all this time, but incredibly it is not. The fragrance hits me the way tropical air does when you first step out of an airport and realize that vacation has begun. I remember picking those raspberries early in the morning before leaving for work, stockpiling them in the freezer until I had enough to make cordial.

They say scent triggers memory more than any other sense. Right behind that first hit of raspberry and nostalgia comes the pressure of other memories. I remember what has changed. I remember the ugly, aluminum-sided building that occupies the space where the raspberry patch used to be and how I still avoid walking past that block. I remember that James moved out just over a year after we shared that raspberry cordial toast with my dad. I remember that I am supposed to be letting go and moving on.

Just as I wish my father would.

I stand staring at the dusty bottle. For one fierce instant I want to swallow every summer day it took to grow the raspberries for that cordial. I want to absorb those days into my bones so that I can never lose them. I take a sip. It tastes like exactly like my memory of it. My eyes sting, but that's as far as I let that go. I carry the bottle back to the kitchen, rinse it out, and place it in the recycling bin.

"I made us a snack," I hear Dad say, and turn to see him holding out a peace offering of toast spread with my raspberry jam.

"Are you sure you don't want to save that for later?" I tease.

"Are you growing raspberries in your new garden?" he asks, smiling.

Dad and me

Raspberry or Blackberry Cordial
Makes approximately 1½ pints

Back when I lived in Ft. Greene and had the community garden adjacent to my back fence and a much bigger apartment, I really got into home winemaking for a while. I even started an email group, WildWines@ yahoogroups.com for fellow enthusiasts. The group is still reportedly a lively one if you are interested in joining.

I don't have room in my current apartment for jugs of wine that won't be ready to bottle until at least a year after they are made, but I do have room to make raspberry cordial. It only requires one wine bottle to ferment in and is ready to drink just four months after you start it. If you get your berries when they are at their peak (and cheapest) in late summer and early fall, you can be toasting your friends with this delicious homebrew by New Year's.

For this recipe it's best to use organically grown or foraged fruit because the recipe depends on wild yeasts for fermentation. Commercially grown fruit has often been sprayed with chemicals and then washed so thoroughly that no wild yeasts remain. Should you need to use commercial fruit, keep an eye on the cordial. If no signs of fermentation are noticeable after 2 days (it should get quite frothy on top), add just a small pinch of wine or baking yeast to kick-start the mixture.

2 quarts fresh or frozen raspberries
2 cups boiling water
2 cups sugar

1. Thaw the berries if using frozen ones. In a non-metal container or crock, crush the berries well with a potato masher or the bottom of a wine bottle. Add the boiling water. This kills off any harmful bacteria but the hardier wine-making yeasts will survive. Cover with cheesecloth or a towel. Leave in a warm place for 24 hours, stirring occasionally.

2. Push the berries and their liquid through a fine sieve, jelly bag or a colander lined with cheesecloth to remove the seeds. Save the juice and discard the pulp.

3. Add the sugar and stir well. Stir again every 15 minutes for 1 hour (5 times total).

4. Strain mixture again through several layers of dampened cheesecloth or a jelly bag. The muslin cloth bags sold to replace plastic bags for fruits and vegetables work well, too.

5. Bottle. Note: at this point some recipes say to cork the bottles tightly. I tried that once. The cordial blew up and shot the corks a good 6 feet and I had raspberry cordial on my ceiling. Instead I recommend sealing the bottles with fermentation locks (available from winemaking suppliers online) or balloons that have been pricked once with a pin. The pinprick allows some of the gasses produced by fermentation to escape so that the balloons don't explode. The balloons will inflate during active fermentation. When they deflate, it is safe to cork your cordial.

6. When fermentation ceases in approximately 2 months, remove the fermentation lock or balloon and cap or cork tightly. Store bottles on their sides in a cool, dark place for an additional 2 months.

7. The cordial may be slightly fizzy when you first open it. Decant before drinking. After decanting, you can store the cordial in clear glass bottles that show off the beautiful color.

Ripe and unripe raspberries in my Brooklyn garden

❧ *The Feral Appetite* ❧

Once while teaching an advanced-level ballet class, I looked up from correcting a student and caught an intense look on the face of a woman watching through the polished glass windows. She was a mom observing her teenage daughter. I could count the bones between her collarbone and her breasts — the mother's, not the dancing daughter's. Well, okay, both of them. The look in the mother's eye was pure hunger. For what, I wondered.

After class the mother invited me to a restaurant nearby where her husband knew the chef. Mother and daughter debated over the menu for a long time. They sat so smugly upright in their size zero jeans. One ordered a salad, the other a boneless, skinless chicken breast with broccoli instead of potatoes. Spitefully, I ordered an overpriced incarnation of mac-and-cheese. Food was standing in for many things at that table. We did not discuss it beyond assuring each other that the chef there was very good. We talked about the improvement in the daughter's pirouettes as if it were the most important thing in the world.

What happens when there is no famine to follow the perpetually available feast? Even a 99-cent special at a fast-food drive-through can have more calories than the homemade meals of earlier times. Both our celebratory feasts and our daily meals have lost the power they once had. In pre-Christian Europe there were rites during which a certain amount of giving-in to excess was expected. In ancient Greece it was the Dionysian nights, in Rome the Bacchanalia. For these events, Dionysius was said to have invented wine in order to give men the lesser madness that prevented the greater madness they could not have survived. After those pagan holidays it was not considered correct to insinuate that anyone had eaten or drunk more than their share. Those were nights for giving in to the lesser madness, making room for it in the midst of otherwise mundane, hard-working lives. The austerity of everyday life balanced the holiday excess and vice versa. Our much less satisfying version is New Year's Eve parties followed by New Year's resolutions.

Somehow I couldn't picture that ballet student or her mother being comfortable on a Dionysian night. I live in a time and place where feasts are guilty pleasures followed by self-imposed famines. In the country I call home, both obesity and anorexia are at an all-time high. How am I supposed to understand "enough"?

There is a look the women in my family get when they are indulging in a forbidden food. Their eyes appear bright and untamed. *I know I'm being bad and I'm going to do it anyway, you can't stop me.* My grandmother sucks the marrow out of a lamb bone with embarrassingly loud noises of pleasure. My mother dunks bread into a bowl of salad dressing; oil runs down her chin. They look up, caught in the act, eyes burnished by mischief. In that instant they resemble wild predatory beasts caught looking up from the kill, bloody from feeding. And just as quickly that primal look is gone from their eyes, replaced by reflexive guilt and bargaining.

Yes, but just one and only after dinner.

I know that look because I get it myself sometimes. Want does a tango with need and emerges as must-have-now. This is not the language of physical hunger, but of something far more complex, a subterranean realm in which I go mad for a moment, truly feeling that I must have something that later turns out to have been a passing craving. In such moments it does no good to remind me of moderation or balance. Moderation does not speak the language of appetite.

"Enough," wrote Caroline Knapp, "Now there's a word that can keep you up at night." Is it enough that I have food to eat and a roof over my head, or do I also need that bigger paycheck, that second glass of wine, those out of season strawberries, the whole pint of ice cream and, while we're at it, a personal trainer to help me atone for all of the above? How much is enough?

I quit cigarettes 3 weeks before James left me, and many friends commented on what great will power and discipline I must have had not to start smoking again during the breakup. They were mistaken. I tried to quit many times using will power and discipline and always failed. What enabled me to quit finally was not will power but desire. I passionately wanted to be the kind of person who was living with the self-esteem and integrity I imagined would result from quitting. I passionately wanted James to think that he hadn't hurt me as badly as he had. I thought, "He'd expect me to start smoking again." So I didn't. It was passion and pride and contrariness, not discipline.

When I danced professionally full time, non-dancers would sometimes say, "You must have such great discipline." There it was again, that assumption of tight control. It was true that I took dance class every day to continually improve my technique and stay in shape, followed that training with hours of rehearsal and then did the evening show. It was true that I showed up to work every day despite injuries, lousy pay, and fatigue. If showing up is discipline, then I had plenty of it. But I'll tell you a secret: there was no discipline involved. Passion, commitment, obsession even, but not discipline. Discipline implies making yourself behave in a way that is contrary to what you truly yearn for. I passionately wanted to dance, and so I did whatever my passion required of me. I was a lover, not a penitent.

When I was 11, I served my parents two tablespoons of dandelion buds sautéed in butter and proclaimed that enough. When I was 16, I guzzled gallons of diet soda because they didn't "count." When James left, I drank a river of wine. As I began creating a new life for myself, I wondered if my appetites could ever be trusted. Habitually denied or redirected, appetites become feral, which is not the same as natural or wild. Feral is the abandoned pet, not the animal born free. It is the stray cat begging to be let in but then hissing at you when you open the door. Feral does not know precisely what it needs, only that it needs something right now. A feral appetite is always sure that there will not be enough, and so it always wants more. In feral appetite I glimpse the origins of a huge, consuming madness, of greed and binges and the peculiar starvation of the spirit that comes from having too much of everything but never enough.

Mary Oliver wrote:
> *You do not have to be good.*
> *You do not have to walk on your knees*
> *For a hundred miles through the desert, repenting.*
> *You only have to let the soft animal of your body*
> *love what it loves…*

Was she right? I passionately wanted what she wrote to be true, and I did trust the strength of my passions. After all it had been passion and commitment more than discipline that had opened every personal and professional door in my life so far.

photo by Tom Caravaglia, 1994
choreography Jennifer Muller

Braised Lamb Shanks
Serves 4

This recipe requires a slow cooker and thanks to that device can be made with very little active kitchen time. It is what my friend Jeff calls an "omigod recipe" because that is what people say when they take their first bite of the rich sauce and tender meat. You won't need knives to eat it with. The meat falls right off the bone. With some rice or potatoes and a salad, you've got yourself a feast.

½ cup red wine
1 tablespoon prepared mustard
2 teaspoons kosher or coarse sea salt
¼ teaspoon ground spicebush berries or allspice
1 teaspoon ground black pepper (optional)
¼ cup dried tomatoes, rehydrated and minced
   OR 2 tsp. tomato paste
5–6 mushrooms, cut into quarters
4 lamb shanks
12 garlic cloves, peeled and crushed (don't panic—it sounds like a lot of garlic but it totally mellows out during the long cooking time)
1 large onion, peeled and chopped into big chunks
1 large carrot, peeled and cut crosswise into ¼-inch rounds
2 sprigs of fresh rosemary,
   leaves stripped away from the woody stems

1. Whisk together the wine, mustard, salt, pepper and spicebush or allspice and pour into the slow cooker.

2. Add the lamb shanks, then the onions, garlic, carrots, and rosemary.

3. Cover and cook on the high setting for 6 hours. With tongs, turn the lamb shanks over. Reduce heat to the low setting and cook for an additional 5 hours.

4. Serve the shanks with some of the juices spooned over the top.

Part Four: The 250

❧ *The 250-Mile Diet* Map ❧

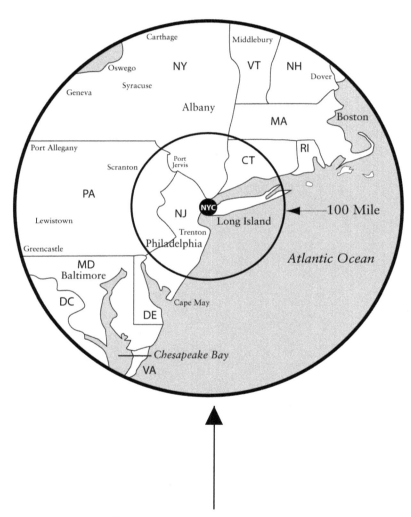

250-mile radius extends from New York City

❦ *An Unexpected Guest* ❦

In the introduction to one of my favorite cooking shows on TV, the voiceover signs off with an invitation to dinner at the chef's house "where one never knows how many people will show up at the table." I have never lived in a home quite like that, but part of me has always wanted to. I can picture myself emerging from the kitchen of my Italian villa, smiling like Diane Lane playing Frances Mayes in *Under the Tuscan Sun*, with a heaped tray of food that smells fabulous. The doorbell rings, I say "Excuse me" to my guests and answer it. Arms fly into the air in surprise and then around each other in joyous welcome. "I didn't know you were coming!" I say, "Your timing is perfect — I'm just about to serve lunch." And of course there is enough in my pantry to feed any number of unexpected guests.

I had an unexpected guest once. I was home alone, writing. The doorbell rang and I hit "save" on my laptop and went to answer it because I thought it might be a late UPS delivery. Instead it was a friend, not a close one, standing outside my apartment door with a bright smile. She explained that she happened to be in my neighborhood and thought it would be fun to stop by and see if I was home. "I mean, why not?" she said, "It's what friends are supposed to do, right?"

There she was, in person, the legendary Unexpected Guest. Now, of course, I was supposed to welcome her into my home and whip up some quick but suitably impressive snack from my pantry. Instead, I was irritated that she'd interrupted the article I'd been working on. I had a deadline. Why hadn't she called first? I was also irritated by how torn I suddenly felt. Why didn't I simply tell her that tonight wasn't a good night for an impromptu visit?

I didn't because at that moment I wanted, deeply and frustratingly, to be the person living the kind of life who would embrace her visit rather than resent it. I wanted to be that Italian chef on TV surrounded by family and friends and completely at ease in the moment, reeking of capability and generosity. I wanted to chuckle warmly and say that I had needed a break from writing anyway. And then I'd expertly throw together our food, maybe with just a dash of showmanship as I flipped an omelet single-handed.

But although my friends and I *do* love to cook for each other, we plan those get-togethers weeks in advance because we are all so overbooked. This gal's arrival slapped me with the unwanted awareness that I was not living in an Italian villa happily welcoming friends and family to my ever-expanding table. I did not feel gracious and glad to see her. I felt middle-aged, stressed and aware that my miniscule apartment hadn't been cleaned recently. I wasn't thinking, "How wonderful to see you!" I was thinking, "Are you out of your mind? Don't you know how busy I am?" I was standing hip deep in the muddy discrepancy between the fantasy-hostess me and real life. And that irritated the hell out of me.

Meanwhile, there she was standing outside my door, starting to look uncomfortable because I hadn't said anything yet. I invited her in, but hedged the invitation by saying that it would have to be a short visit because I needed to get back to writing.

My living room is also my kitchen, so she could watch from her seat on the sofa as I opened a cabinet over the sink and took down a jar of home-canned dilly beans. The scent of the bay, dill, garlic and thyme I make them with filled the room as soon as I opened the jar and drained the beans in a colander for an instant salad. I felt a little lighter as I put a dish of them down on the coffee table in front of her. You see, I said to an invisible panel of TV-cooking-show judges, I really do keep a well-stocked pantry…just in case reality ever catches up with my dreams.

I planned to kick her out after no more than 20 minutes, but we started talking about our lives, catching up, and the conversation lasted well over an hour. As we munched on the dilly beans I told her about a time when that particular pickle had gotten me out of paying an electrician's bill.

The electrician's name was Joe and his method of testing the faulty wiring was to lick his finger, touch the wires, then jump away shouting, "Yup, that's live." At one point he commented on how old the wiring in my basement apartment was.

"Twenty-four!" he exclaimed.

"Years old?" I asked

"No, 1924, I'm guessing."

Then he noticed the jars of homemade preserves lined up on my shelves in the hallway.

"So who does all the canning?" he asked.

"I do," I replied.

"Get outta here!" His focus slipped far away and he smiled a little. "My aunt used to make the best dilly beans. You ever try those? That was in Virginia." He looked at my shelves again, and shook his head appreciatively. "Her dilly beans sure were good."

As he was finishing up, I handed him a jar of my dilly beans and enjoyed his grin. After he left I looked at the bill he handed me and it was blank. I called the next day to ask what I owed him. "Those beans sure were good," he said.

My unexpected guest laughed at the story. "I should probably let you get back to work," she said. But after she left I didn't go back to work immediately. I sat nibbling on the last few dilly beans and thinking how pleasant the evening had turned out to be after all. I thought about that electrician and how his visit, too, had turned into something worth smiling about.

Every summer when green beans come into season I buy a few extra pounds of them at the farmers market, many more than I can eat myself. I think of Joe the Electrician and his aunt in Virginia, and the friend who stopped by when I was too busy for her, and I go home and make a big batch of dilly beans. To have on hand, you know, just in case.

Dilly Beans
Makes 1 pint jar

Dilly beans are one of the easiest pickles to make, and you can use this same brine and method with other vegetables, including cucumber spears, carrots, and bell peppers. You don't have to make a lot of jars of them at a time: the recipe below is for a single pint jar. They need to be processed in a boiling water bath in canning jars for long-term shelf storage, but if you have the refrigerator space they'll last in there for at least 4 months. Canned or refrigerated, be sure to leave them alone for at least 3 weeks before tasting; the vinegar taste will mellow and the herbs infuse their flavor into the vegetables during that time. Do not reduce the amount of vinegar in the recipe or they will not be safely preserved.

> **Approximately 2 cups green or wax beans, washed and trimmed to fit jar lengthwise**
> **¾ cup wine vinegar**
> **½ cup water**
> **½ teaspoon kosher salt**
> **1 teaspoon honey**
> **1 sprig dill leaves or 1 dill flowerhead**
> **1 bay leaf**
> **1 sprig thyme**
> **1 small hot pepper, fresh or dried**
> **1 clove garlic, peeled**
> **Approximately 2 tablespoons olive oil**

1. Tightly pack beans into a clean 1-pint canning jar. It is easier to lay the beans in lengthwise if you put the jar on its side and slide the beans in that way. Add the herbs, pepper and garlic as you go, placing the prettier ones like red chile pepper or bay leaf between the beans and the sides of the jar where they will show.

2. Bring the vinegar, water, honey and salt to a boil. Pour over the other ingredients.

3. Top with olive oil to cover the surface, still leaving 1/2-inch head room.

4. Process in a boiling water bath for 10 minutes.

Also, please see my links from About.com:
http://foodpreservation.about.com/od/Green-or-Wax-Bean-Pickles/r/
Dilly-Beans-Recipe.htm

HOW TO PROCESS IN A BOILING WATER BATH

A boiling water bath is great because you don't need a pressure canner or other special equipment, but a boiling water bath can only be safely used for recipes and ingredients that are acidic, such as pickles and fruits. Low-acid vegetables and recipes must be pressure canned rather than processed in a boiling water bath. But with a vinegar pickle such as dilly beans it is completely safe to use a boiling water bath. Just make sure you are using a vinegar that has at least 4.5% acidity (most commercial vinegars do—check the labels) and don't reduce the amount of vinegar in the recipe to less than 50% water and 50% vinegar. If that is still too sharp tasting for you, add a little more sugar.

All you need is a canning jar with a lid that will form an airtight seal when processed (available at most hardware and houseware stores, or online at www.homecanning.com), and a pot deep enough for the jar to be covered by at least 1 inch of water. A stockpot works beautifully. Even better is one of those pasta pots with the removable colander. You need something to keep the jar off of the bottom of the pot so it doesn't crack. This can be accomplished with the pasta pot colander, or a rack that fits inside the pot, or a dishtowel placed under the jars.

Very short processing times such as the 5 minutes usually recommended for jellies require sterilizing jars before filling them. For the dilly bean recipe you do not need to sterilize the jar first because it will be processed for 10 full minutes. But do make sure the jar is clean. Follow the recipe, checking to make sure that the beans are completely covered by the liquid and that there is at least half an inch of air space between the liquid and the rim of the jar (without this "headspace" the lid won't seal). Wipe the rim of the jar dry with a clean towel. Put on the lid and screw the band just until finger-tight.

Place the jar on your rack or towel in the pot and add enough water to cover the top of the jar by at least 1 inch. Bring to a boil. Start timing according to the recipe instructions once the water is at a full roiling boil (10 minutes for dilly beans). When the time is up, remove the jar to someplace it can cool for several hours until it is completely cooled. Jostling it during that time could cause the jar to lose its seal.

You will hear a click or a ping as the lid's center goes from convex and flexible to concave and firm. When you press down on the lid now it won't move, whereas unprocessed lids do. Store at room temperature out of direct light for up to 1 year. The food will still be safe after a year, but the quality starts to decline. If for any reason your jar doesn't seal, store in the refrigerator and eat the contents within 2 to 4 weeks. Or you could try reprocessing with a fresh lid.

❦ *The 250* ❦

*"...to live now as you think human beings should live,
in defiance of all that is bad around us,
is itself a marvelous victory."*
—Howard Zinn

One week before my 45th birthday I started a blog called Leda's Urban Homestead and announced that I would be starting a year long 250-Mile Diet. This is how I explained it in my first post:

"On August 7th I will begin a year of living almost exclusively on foods grown or raised within a 250-mile radius from my home in Brooklyn, NY.

Local is the new organic according to the press, but to be honest I was into it back when most people thought refusing to eat an out of season tomato was just weird. So this year, inspired by several excellent books written by locavores, including Gary Nabhan's *Coming Home To Eat*, Barbara Kingsolver's *Animal, Vegetable, Miracle*, Alisa Smith and J.B. Mackinnon's *Plenty*, and Michael Pollan's *The Omnivore's Dilemma* I've decided to take my personal enthusiasm for eating locally to the next level.

Why 250 miles? Well, I ruled out the more extreme 100-mile diet that Smith and Mackinnon did because my CSA share comes from a farm that is close to 200 miles away. I am just not willing to abandon farmer Ted Blomgren of Windflower Farms after several years of eating what he grows. I chose 250 because that is the number of miles Nabhan allowed himself during his year of eating locally, and on the justification that that is approximately the number of miles most farm trucks can travel on one tank of gas.

Why I think this will be fun at least most of the time: I love making personal connections to the food that is about to make the most personal of journeys to become part of me. And I love to cook, so this is not about a year of hardship. I won't give myself any brownie points for suffering during this year of local food. Quite the opposite!

I'll be sharing recipes, links and tips here, and my hope is that this blog will be a useful resource and inspiration for your own local eating adventures."

The day before I began The 250 I threw a birthday party for myself. It was a lovely August evening and most of the food was local, seasonal stuff even though The 250 hadn't officially started yet. I sat in the garden with friends and answered questions that would become increasingly familiar as the year went on: What about chocolate? What are you going to do in winter? What about when you travel? If you get local eggs but the chicken was fed non-local grain, can you still eat them? What about spices? Olive oil? Sugar?

To answer some of those questions for myself as well as for my friends, I posted The Rules online:

"1. **All food to be sourced from within a 250-mile radius of Park Slope, Brooklyn, NY, USA except as noted below.**

2. **OK to use up non-local ingredients on hand as of the decision to do this experiment. Not OK to stock up before start date on August 7th, nor to restock non-local items if I run out before the end date of The 250-Mile Diet Year.**

3. **I am allowed three 'Trade Items,' a.k.a. non-local ingredients, that I am going to continue using this year: olive oil, coffee, and salt. All Trade Items should be organic whenever possible and sourced as locally as possible.** *

4. **Rules are suspended when I'm invited by friends to dine with them, either at a restaurant or at their home. However, this exemption cannot be applied more than twice a month. The rest of the time, you're coming over to my place for a 250-mile meal.**

5. **OK to accept and eat homemade food gifts that contain non-local ingredients. Wasting food is not the point of The 250, and did you really think I was going to turn down Ellen's homemade preserves just because she used imported cane sugar to make them? However, this rule is not an attempt to solicit boxes of chocolate or other items you think I am going to die without.**

If I were doing The 250 in my old home in Park Slope, Brooklyn now, I wouldn't need to give myself the salt exemption. Urban Sproule is producing sea salt from water harvested off the coast of Long Island and solar-dried on a Manhattan rooftop.

6. Rules are suspended when traveling, but on the road I should try to eat locally produced foods whenever possible.

7. OK to bring back foods that were produced within 100 miles of a place I visit while traveling. This means I can bring home organically grown olive oil and Meyer lemons from California when I visit my family there in December. Yay. However, not OK to stock up quantity. Only what I can carry home with me. No overweight luggage charges at the airport. I chose 100 miles for this Rule instead of 250 because when overseas 250 miles could include an entire country. That seems a little too generous a definition of 'local'."

One woman wrote to me, "Why this limit? Our ancestors walked up to 1500 miles for choice edibles!"

I replied:

"Exactly: they walked. The environmental impact of walking is very different from the impact of shipping food that same distance in gas-guzzling trucks and airplanes. I want to minimize the amount of petroleum fuel used to bring food to me and I want to support the local economy and small local farms. I also enjoy getting to know the farmers who grow my food. That kind of direct connection to people and planet is not common when you live in the city, as I have for most of my life. And yes, the ultimate local food comes from the wild edible plants I forage and those I grow in my garden, but my garden is very small!

Other reasons for my extreme local eating year include the deliciousness of the food, picked in its prime and just before I buy it—so much fresher than shipped food! I am learning new skills from this experiment, including making sourdough starter from my backyard grapes (and keeping it going because I don't have commercial yeast to bake with). There is a wonderful sense of coming home in all of this, of finding out what here tastes like.

I am not a purist about it, and I do allow myself some exemptions including salt and olive oil. And at the end of this 250-mile year I'm sure I will again eat California-or-Florida grown citrus and avocados and other imported foods...occasionally, as special treats and with full appreciation of the true cost of bringing them all those miles to my table.

In the meantime, the articles I have written about my experience so far have inspired other people to pay more attention to where their food comes from and the impact of their food choices on the environment. Several farmers have written to thank me for sending local customers their way who might not have known about their products otherwise. All of that brings me great joy. Last but not least, it is fun for me."

When I started The 250, I was more worried about what I'd be missing than what I'd find. One by one I ran out of the exotic, imported ingredients that I'd taken for granted before. I obsessed over the lack of citrus and the fact that none of the vinegars in any of the stores I visited were from anywhere closer than California. What was I going to do for sourness in salad dressings and tangy sauces? I did eventually find a source of local vinegar, but meanwhile I'd already taught myself how to make my own from a recipe I found online (see page 86).

I wasn't worried that I'd starve. I was worried that I'd be limited to bland, repetitive food. Sugar, black pepper, cinnamon, ginger, soy sauce, and lemons are not about nourishment. They are about flavor and variety. I started foraging more than ever before, stocking up on wild spicebush berries (*Lindera benzoin*) to use instead of allspice,*peppergrass (*Lepidium spp.*) seeds to use when I ran out of black pepper, and wild ginger (*Asarum canadense*, no relation to the Indonesian plant that commercial ginger comes from). I froze cornelian cherry (*Cornus mas*) and Japanese knotweed (*Polygonum cuspidatum*) juice for their sourness to supplement my homemade vinegar. For citrus-y flavor, I grew and dried lemon verbena, lemongrass, lemon thyme, lemon basil, and lemon balm in the garden.

Eventually, I noticed that all this experimenting with alternative seasonings was making my meals more flavorful than ever. I also noticed that summer was about to be autumn and I needed to stock up for winter. I couldn't remember what would be available at the farmers' markets in January. I'd shopped at them in winter but I hadn't really paid attention. There would be apples, I was pretty sure, and probably root vegetables, but I didn't know what else. In winter, my CSA farm share would go from being a weekly delivery to a monthly box that would definitely not last 4 weeks, so for most of my food I'd be dependent on the farmers' markets and what was in my pantry. The dilly beans and pretty gift jars

---

*I no longer agree with my old field guides that spicebush tastes "like allspice." It's true that you can use it in similar recipes and amounts, but expect a unique flavor that has peppery and floral notes allspice lacks.

of jellies I'd made in the past had been a hobby, but once The 250 began I got serious and started canning in quantity. The food dehydrator on a corner of my living room floor hummed nonstop for a couple of months.

There isn't really a pantry in my apartment. Actually, I don't even have a kitchen — it's just one side of the living room that is also my dining room. So I quickly ran out of space for all the jars of food I was amassing. One day I was at a hardware store and saw some plastic bins labeled for under-the-bed storage. Aha! They were exactly the right height for my pint jars, and just barely fit under my fold-out futon. The first night that I slept with food under my bed I had an attack of the giggles. Except for the jazz music coming through my window from the club next door, and the sound of a couple arguing in the apartment above mine, I could almost pretend I was living in a one-room cabin out in the woods with every nook filled with winter survival supplies. I remembered all my childhood fantasies of running away to live off the land and that made me laugh harder. This was definitely not business as usual in New York City.

Once winter arrived I learned that the one leafy vegetable I could count on getting was cold-hardy cabbage. I didn't mind cabbage, but it wasn't a favorite food, and I wasn't used to eating it almost every day. I made sauerkraut in pint jars until my CSA gave me a big fermentation crock as a thank-you for being their sole site coordinator for several months. It was tall, dark brown and glossy, a handsome thing that looked like it could have been décor in someone's weekend home in the country. But in my home, it had to be functional as well as comely. I looked for somewhere in my apartment that it could sit for weeks while cabbage after cabbage bubbled away en route to becoming sauerkraut. The only place I had room was a corner of my bedroom. Now I was sleeping with about fifty jars of food under my bed and a crock in the corner that burped loudly every few minutes.

I really didn't know how much food one person needed to get through a winter. I'd canned tomatoes before, but when I ran out of the homemade version I just went to the store and picked up a can of Muir Glen organic tomatoes. I wouldn't be able to do that during The 250. I was guessing blindly at what was probably common knowledge a few generations ago. I estimated 1 pint of tomatoes per week to last until the next tomatoes ripened in my garden in late July.

Six months into The 250 I wasn't obsessing about what I was missing anymore. I didn't even glance at the packaged food on the shelves when I went to the store to buy cat food (my cat, G.T., did not do the 250-mile diet with me, unless you count the mouse she proudly caught that December). I walked by the piles of out-of-season eggplants and corn from South America and they looked alien to me. What I was eating at home was much more interesting. I even invented some fun recipes to use up all of that sauerkraut.

But people kept asking about what I was missing. I got irritated explaining over and over that I wasn't suffering. Finally, I posted this on my blog:

"If I came back from a trip to Italy you wouldn't exclaim, 'But didn't you miss burgers and fries?' Instead, we'd talk about all the fabulous food I ate while traveling through the regions of that country, each with a unique cuisine based on local ingredients. Yet when I tell people that I am eating a diet based on what is produced close to my home in Brooklyn the first thing they want to talk about is all the things I am deprived of: 'No sugar, no cashews, no citrus, no peanut butter, no bananas, no...! For a whole year?'

Well, focusing on what I can't have is dramatic, but the truth is that I have never eaten so well.

I've stopped trying to replicate the flavors I was used to with substitutions (local honey for sugar, etc.). Instead I cook to discover the most delicious way to use what I have. That is, after all, how every regional cuisine was invented. That is why the classic recipes of Brittany rely on butter but it's all about olive oil in Provence — because that is what they had.

So please, no more questions about whether I am suffering on my 250-mile diet. Instead, pretend I am traveling someplace that has really fantastic food.

Ask me what here tastes like."

UPDATE: The 250 was a game-changer for me. It connected me to a community of inspired, motivated, and radically kind rebels interested in creating real solutions for a sustainable food system. We weren't going to wait around for the Monsanto alumni now holding government jobs to fix things; we were already trying to live the solution(s).

This wasn't the back to the land movement of my parents' generation, although certainly we owed much to that generation. But most of us stayed in the city. My new friends raised chickens in their Brooklyn backyards, foraged beside me in the parks, raised bees and vegetables on Manhattan rooftops. We taught (and still teach) workshops and wrote (and still write) books to share skills, contacts, information...not to mention heaps of delicious food.

Many positive changes occurred. It is so much easier to find locally grown ingredients than it was back when I did The 250. "Local" has become a mainstream buzzword, almost as popular as "organic." The number of farmers markets, CSAs, coops, and food share programs has exploded in many parts of North America and in other countries as well.

But there is still such a very long way to go. Industrial agriculture with its toxic chemicals and topsoil-destroying ways, with its insufficiently tested Genetically Modified Organisms (GMOs) and its hormone-pumped, claustrophobic, and resource-wasting animal factories...That is still the dangerous norm. According to the Research Program on Climate Change, Agriculture and Food Security "Food production and consumption contribute 19 to 29 percent of total greenhouse gas emissions." It is impossible to tackle climate change acceleration without a complete overhaul of the dominant agricultural system.

When I read my notes on The 250 now they sound well-intentioned but naive. As often happens, the "revolution" began with high spirits and an unrealistic time frame. Although global warming is progressing faster than originally predicted by most scientists, changing human habits is taking longer than some of us hoped. Unfortunately, time is one of the things that is rapidly running out (along with the polar ice caps, the half-drowned Maldives islands, petroleum, and many other parts of the world as we knew it).

But I didn't write this book to depress anyone. Quite the opposite. The stresses on the planetary system as it currently exists are intensifying, and our food choices may have even more of an impact now than they did a few years ago. That empowers us as eaters to make a real difference. The beautiful reality is still that the ways of producing food that are the healthiest for the environment are also the healthiest for us...and they are also much more pleasurable to prepare, to share, and to eat.

Saurerkraut in a Jar

Makes 1 pint jar

Real sauerkraut isn't the harsh-tasting stuff preserved with vinegar that you buy in a can. It is crunchy with a mildly sour fresh taste. What preserves it is a natural process called lactic fermentation. Salt is used to prevent harmful bacteria during the process. Meanwhile, salt-tolerant good-for-you bacteria start the fermentation process that eventually results in a pickle. This is exactly the process that true kosher dill pickles are made by.

Lacto-fermented foods are high in vitamin C (in the 18th century, Captain Cook prevented his crew from getting scurvy by feeding them sauerkraut). They are also rich in probiotics that do wonders for your digestive and immune systems.

You can lacto-ferment almost any vegetable, and you don't need a crock (although crocks are cool and use yours if you have one). The recipe below is for a single jar of sauerkraut.

> **About 3 cups finely shredded cabbage**
> **1to 2 tablespoons kosher or other non-iodized salt**
> **¼ teaspoon caraway seeds (optional but traditional)**
> **2 to 3 juniper berries (ditto)**
> **A clean, wide-mouth glass pint jar and lid**

1. Pack the cabbage into the jar one layer at a time, sprinkling with 1 tablespoon of the salt and adding the spices as you go. Press down hard to release the cabbage juices. Stop 1 inch from the rim. Wait an hour while the salt draws out the cabbage juices. If there are not enough juices to completely cover the cabbage, pour in a brine made by dissolving 1 tablespoon of salt in a cup of filtered water. Filtered is important because the chlorine that is added to most tap water can prevent the lactic fermentation from occurring. Make sure to leave 1 inch of headroom between the kraut and the rim of the jar.

2. Cover and leave the jar at room temperature for at least 3 days but up to 1 week. Every day, use a spoon to skim off any bubbly scum that appears on the surface. The scum is actually a good sign; it means that fermentation is under way. But it's not something you want to eat in the final product.

3. At this point, your sauerkraut should have a mildly tangy smell and taste. If by some chance it smells at all "off," discard it (but it won't if you've followed the recipe). Store sauerkraut in the refrigerator, or a cool, dark cellar if you are lucky enough to have one. It will keep for up to 1 year.

One note: lacto-fermentation works best at temperatures below 70 degrees. If you must make yours in a warmer environment than that, add an extra teaspoon of salt to the jar.

Saurerkraut and Apple Salad
Makes 2 large or 4 small servings

---

1 cup homemade sauerkraut
2 apples, peeled and finely chopped
1 carrot, peeled and grated
½ medium red onion, peeled and finely sliced
2 tablespoons toasted pumpkin seeds

1. Toss all together except the seeds and let sit 15 minutes for the flavors to "marry" before serving. Sprinkle seeds on top.

That's it: the brine clinging to the sauerkraut provides all the dressing this salad needs. However, if you are not on a local-foods-only restricted diet, or if sesame grows where you live, adding a half a teaspoon of toasted sesame oil is a delicious variation.

WHAT IS A CSA?

CSA stands for Community Supported Agriculture. Members of a CSA pay a farmer up front at the beginning of the year for fruits and vegetables that the farmer will deliver weekly during the growing season. This gives the farmer money when he or she needs it to buy seed, repair equipment, etc. The members share the risks of the season with the farmer. In a good year, the bounty of the weekly shares may be almost more than a family of four can use up. If hailstorms or other natural disasters strike, then the shares will be smaller even though the price is the same. This gives the farmer a buffer to stay in business even when nature isn't cooperating. What the members get is super-fresh produce picked at its peak and the chance to meet the person producing their food. There is no middleman. Many CSAs also offer honey, meat, eggs, cheese, cut flowers and other locally produced products. To find out if there is a CSA in your neighborhood, or how to start one, please see the Useful Resources appendix.

❧ *Coming Into Flour* ❧

Until I didn't have any, I hadn't given dry beans much thought. In early fall of my local eating challenge year shell beans showed up at the farmers' markets. Since shell beans left on the vine eventually become dry beans, I expected to see those soon, too, but they never materialized. I wanted to make a Portugese-style soup for which beans are essential. I also missed hummus, the Middle Eastern dip usually made with chickpeas but which I figured I could substitute any other bean for.

I Googled "New York grown dry beans" and every other way of phrasing the search that I could come up with. I kept getting web sites that started with the depressing sentence, "New York State used to be the leading producer of dry beans…"

Finally one day in December I went to a special event called Wintermarket. It was snowing hard and the vendors and farmers and celeb chef Mario Batali, bless them, were standing outside under the awning of the former Fulton Fish Market. And there on one of the tables were white beans and pinto beans and black beans. Yay! I bought a pound of each and got the name of the grower, Cayuga Pure Organics. I emailed Cayuga that night thinking my bean woes were past.

The farmer was very supportive of my local eating commitment and eager to find ways to sell his beans in New York City. But he was having a tough time doing so because beans are ubiquitous and cheap and heavy (think shipping cost) and nobody really thinks about them until, well, until they do. The price for anything less than a hundred pounds was more than double what even organic beans cost in the stores, but he offered me the wholesale price if I could put together a 100-pound order. So I posted on my blog and emailed my CSA asking if anyone was interested in going in with me on an order of locally grown, organic beans. Two weeks later I had four 25-pound bags of beans in my hallway and a stream of people coming by to pick up their share of the order.

The beans were delicious, with a shorter cooking time than those dusty bags of Goya pebbles on the supermarket shelf or anything in a can. Turns out that the older dry beans are, the longer they take to cook, even after an overnight soak. Beans from a recent harvest still contain enough moisture to support the embryonic seed within, even though they appear to be dry. After soaking my first batch of local black beans overnight, as most recipes say to, I had to run to work and didn't get around to checking on them until that evening. They had sprouted.

Another ubiquitous staple that was hard to find and led me on a treasure hunt was flour. When I started The 250, I didn't know if I'd be able to get local grain products. I thought of wheat as something that grew in the Midwest, not the rocky soil of the Northeast. The hunt for local flour was a major quest in Smith and Mackinnon's book on local eating, so I knew it might not be easy. I went to the information stall at the Union Square Greenmarket in Manhattan and asked if any of the farmers were doing grains. I got a scribbled handwritten note of a few farmers who were sometimes, but not always, at the market.

After a couple of weeks, one of the farmers finally emailed me back (I never heard from the others). Yes, wheat and other grains are grown in New York and milled into flour and he had them, but he was only at the market half the year. It wasn't that part of the year. But he wrote that if I emailed my order to him by Thursday I could pick it up on Saturday at the stall of another farmer. I had to enclose a check or cash in a sealed envelope with both my name and his written on its front. I would then hand this envelope over to someone at this other farmer's stall and "they'll have something for you." Mind you, since we were talking about flour, what they were going to hand me would be a bag of white powder. I was having serious '80s flashbacks. The reason for this clandestine delivery method was that Greenmarket rules require the vendors at each stall to be from the farm that produced the products for sale. A good rule most of the time, but I think it may have made my miller's life unnecessarily complicated (and mine). I started thinking of it as "007 flour." I showed up on Saturday, handed over my envelope, and was in possession of all the future bread and pasta a gal could want.

Just as with those unexpectedly sprouted beans, there was a learning curve with this flour. It, too, was fresher than anything I was accustomed to. That threw all of my recipes off. Every dough or batter I made was too wet if I stuck to a recipe. I had to learn how to tell by look and feel when it was right rather than relying on my measuring cups.

That was frustrating at first, but then it got interesting. It reminded me of a time when I asked my Grandma Nea how long *horta* needed to cook. She answered, "Until it's done." That kind of grandma know-how isn't part of the education most of us get nowadays, certainly not any I got. Cookbooks and Food Network stars tell us exactly how much of each ingredient to use and how long a recipe takes not only to cook but to prep (how can they know how fast I chop I wonder?). That's swell if you're using standardized ingredients. But what if your flour doesn't need as much liquid as Pillsbury's? How will you know that even though you followed the recipe exactly your pancake batter is too wet and you need to add more flour?

I was excited when I realized that I *did* know, that the longer I worked with local foods the less I needed recipes. I just had to pay attention and be willing to bake a few leaden doorstops on the way to a perfect loaf of bread. And when I did finally make that perfect loaf it was more than good, it was a triumph, because I knew exactly how much trial and error had gone into making it.

I lived a daily treasure hunt, each new ingredient a prize to celebrate. And the food gave me an education in skills that can't be learned from a book. I didn't have my grandmother looking over my shoulder to tell me when I'd done it right. I was becoming my own grandmother.

I looked for, and found, new ingredients in unexpected places. Once I bought raw honey from a botanical garden on Long Island when I was there for a day as the guest speaker. The beehive was within view of the conference room where I spoke. Another time I found butter made from local milk tucked in between the supermarket brands at a small, somewhat dilapidated corner store. Just walking down the street with the idea that I might discover a new local ingredient made me smile and bounce a little as I walked.

Forager's eyes, that's what this feeling reminded me of. Ever since I was a kid collecting dandelion buds in the park I've kept an eye on the plants I walk by. There might be a great find right around the corner: a mulberry tree loaded with fruit leaning over a fence, fat Japanese knotweed stalks at the perfect moment for harvesting, black walnuts dropping onto the sidewalk. It's a perk of knowing how to identify edible plants and mushrooms that I find gourmet ones for free even in the middle of the city. Often I've shared the excitement of an especially fabulous find with my friend Ellen, who has become a formidable forager herself.

Text message to Ellen:

"Found Hen on way to teach ballet at Adelphi. No time. Will come back."

Reply 30 seconds later: **"I'm jealous! Hope it will still be there."**

The "hen" I'd found was a wild edible mushroom, hen-of-the-woods a.k.a Maitake, a.k.a. *Grifola frondosa*. It is one of the yummiest wild mushrooms out there and you can buy it for a painfully high price at high-end markets. I might be about to score several pounds of gourmet treat for free if it was still there on my way back to the train.

I taught my 9 a.m. ballet class and then my 10:30 a.m. modern dance class and I even managed to get half of a solo choreographed for the new piece I was working on, but I kept thinking about whether or not that hen would still be there. Finally, it was time to head back to the train station and I ran to that particular oak tree. The hen was still there. I rummaged through my backpack past the ballet shoes and sweaty leotard looking for the harvesting knife I always carry just in case (doesn't everyone?). I cut the mushroom, at least a foot in diameter, off at the base and stashed it in what had been my lunch bag. But first I took a photo of it with my phone and sent it to Ellen along with the message, **"Got it!"**

The treasure hunt aspect of foraging was something I always enjoyed, and now I was getting to shop for my "regular" food with the same sharp enthusiast's eyes. I was eating wonderful food, learning new skills, making the most of my foraging know-how, minimizing my impact on the environment, supporting the local economy and small organic farms, and having some serious fun.

The first time I came home with several pounds of 007 flour, I added this signature line to my blog:

WHY EAT LOCAL?
BECAUSE SAVING THE WORLD TASTES GOOD.

Portuguese-Style Kale and Bean Soup
Serves 4 (or one hungry person for several days)

---

1 large bunch of kale, thick midribs removed, coarsely chopped
8 ounces sausage (optional), in approximately one-inch pieces
1 medium onion, peeled and chopped
4 cloves garlic, peeled and chopped
1½ tablespoons olive oil
1 to 2 small dried hot peppers, crushed
2 cups cooked beans, preferably small white ones
2 medium potatoes, scrubbed and cut into 1-inch chunks
¼ cup dry white wine
1 quart chicken or vegetable stock
Salt

1. Heat ½ tablespoon of the olive oil over medium-high heat in a large pot. Add the sausage if using and cook until browned on all sides. Remove the sausage and set aside.

2. Reduce heat to medium-low and add the remaining tablespoon of oil. Add the onions and sauté until soft and starting to color. Add the garlic and hot pepper and stir for one minute.

3. Pour in the wine and simmer for 1 minute.

4. Add the potatoes and the stock and raise the heat. Bring to a boil then reduce heat and simmer, uncovered, until the potatoes are just barely cooked through, 10 to 15 minutes.

5. Add the kale a handful at a time until it all wilts. Simmer, covered, 10 minutes more.

6. Add the cooked beans and salt to taste. Turn off the heat, cover, and let sit for at least half an hour for the flavors to develop (this soup is even better the next day). Reheat and serve with a crusty, chewy loaf of bread.

Basic Pancakes

(and learning how to tell when your batter is right even if it's different from the recipe)

Makes at least 16 pancakes, maybe more, depending on your flour. See note in Sourdough Pancake recipe below about freezing leftover pancakes.

There are measurements in the recipe below, but note the range from 1 to 2½ cups of flour possibly needed. I'll talk you through it.

> 1 to 2½ cups flour
> 2 tablespoons honey
> 1¾ tablespoons baking powder
> 1 teaspoon salt
> 1½ cups milk
>   OR 1 cup recently refreshed sourdough starter plus ½ cup milk
> 3 tablespoons butter, melted,
>   plus additional for greasing the pan or griddle
> 2 eggs, beaten

1. Heat a griddle or nonstick pan heated over medium-high heat. It is hot enough when a sprinkle of water "dances" and sputters on the surface.

2. Whisk the dry ingredients together, starting with just 1 cup of the flour.

3. In a separate bowl, whisk the wet ingredients together.

4. Add the wet ingredients to the dry ingredients. Stir to combine, but don't stir so much that it's perfectly smooth. You want there to still be some lumps in the batter.

5. How to know if you need to add more flour? Pancake batter should look like a milkshake with some lumps in it. Not a super-thick, frosty milkshake, but thicker than, say, chocolate milk. Add any additional flour, no more than ¼ cup at a time.

6. Spread a little butter on the pan or griddle to grease it. Ladle out about ¼ cup of batter for each pancake.

7. Let cook on the first side until all the bubbles on the surface have popped and the edges are turning golden. The surface will go from being glossy to matte. Flip. Cook on the second side half as long as the first side took. Serve immediately, or keep warm in a 200°F oven while you work on the rest of the pancakes. You may need to grease the pan or griddle with a little more butter or oil in between each batch.

Sourdough Pancakes
Makes 12 to 16 pancakes

These are my hands-down favorite pancakes, with a wonderful springy texture and slightly tangy flavor. But they do require a bit more planning because you have to start them the night before you are going to cook them. The actual active time in the kitchen is about the same as for the Basic Pancake recipe.

This batter doesn't keep well, nor can you cut the recipe in half easily (half an egg?). If 12 to 16 is more pancakes than you need, go ahead and make all of them, let the ones you don't eat right away cool completely, then freeze between sheets of wax or parchment paper inside freezer bags or containers. No need to thaw, just pop them into a 250°F oven until warmed through for a quick breakfast.

1 cup recently refreshed sourdough starter (see page 47)
1 to 2 cups flour
1 cup milk
1 egg, beaten
2 teaspoons melted butter, plus more for the griddle or skillet
1 teaspoon baking soda
1 teaspoon baking powder
½ teaspoon salt
1 tablespoon honey

1. The night before you will be serving these pancakes, mix the sourdough starter with 1 cup of the flour and the milk in a non-reactive mixing bowl. Cover and leave until morning.

2. Mix in the egg, melted butter, honey, salt, baking soda, and baking powder. Stir to combine, but don't stir so much that it's perfectly smooth. You want there to still be some lumps in the batter. You may need to add more flour depending on how liquid your sourdough starter was. Add any additional flour no more than ¼ cup at a time. Pancake batter should look like a milkshake with some lumps in it. Not a super-thick, frosty milkshake, but thicker than, say, chocolate milk.

3. Proceed with Steps 6 and 7 of the Basic Pancake recipe above.

❧ *Samara* ❧

(A samara is a winged seed, technically a dry dehiscent fruit, such as a maple seed, or "key." It is aerodynamic so that it can travel far from the parent tree and put down roots someplace that provides enough soil and sunlight for it to thrive.)

Before The 250, I was getting restless. I missed the tours of my performing years. I missed performing. I still had attacks of grieving for my marriage and the Greene Avenue garden, and I was so bored with that, but nothing I tried sped up the healing process. Everything about New York City annoyed me: I was annoyed by the way teenaged boys sprawled across two seats each on the subway while I stood, by having to work too many hours to pay the rent, by the Botox babes on the Upper East Side, by the Northeastern winter in general. I told my mom that I was going to buy a round-the-world ticket and spend a year on the road, traveling west from Australia in December. If I planned it right, traveling west the entire time and ending up in South America, it would be soft, sultry summer wherever I was. The Year of Summer sounded like a grand plan and possibly a book waiting to be written.

But I didn't have the money to go on an extended trip. One frigid night when the heat and hot water were out in my apartment building and I was feeling sorry for myself, I picked up the phone and said yes to a short trip that I'd been invited on months earlier. I joined a small group traveling to Brazil with life coach Meike Fruchtenicht and health counselor Jena La Flamme. We spent a night in Rio and then moved on to Ilha Grande, an island just off the coast of Brazil. We were on vacation but also getting lots of coaching and exercise and hoping to come back healthier and with a new plan for our lives. I was ready for a new plan.

We left in February, just when winter was driving me crazy. The house where we stayed was a steep 20-minute hike up from the town and the beach below. It had an outdoor patio area with a roof but no walls and a large, rectangular table. There were no other buildings in view, just palm trees and sky. We sat at that table after dinner each night, with candles as our only light source, surrounded by the humid Brazilian night. And we got coached, one at a time.

I told Meike I wanted more freedom in my life and I wanted to be an entrepreneur, to be my own boss. She asked me for a tangible symbol, a marker that would also be a practical, specific something to work on right away. "Something that will let you know you have made these changes we are talking about tonight," she said. I imagined a book I would write. When I told Meike that, she said, "Good, so you'll write a chapter and read it to us tomorrow night."

Every day for the rest of our week on Ilha Grande I wrote. I wrote at the beach and beside waterfalls and on the ferry. And every night I brought my laptop to the big candlelit table and read what I had written that day to the others. From the start, the stories I wanted to tell were about food and nature, what those meant to me, and how sometimes they had been the only things that kept me going.

After I read, the conversations lasted late into the night. We talked about longing for the sense of connection that I sometimes found through food and plants. The others said it was bizarrely unrelated that I also had a dance career, and I said no, not at all. Dance, to me, was about communication with and connection to the audience. Connection to where my food comes from, connection to an audience, connection to nature even in the city — it all felt like the same thing to me. We traded story after story about how disconnected from nature and each other we'd become.

One of the stories I told was about a moment during the power blackout of 2003. My local supermarket lowered its collapsible metal fence early and the owner told me later that he'd feared the kind of looting that had happened back in the blackouts of the '70s. Like most people in my neighborhood, when I saw that he'd closed shop I headed to the deli on the corner to stock up on food and bottled water. There was a long line but the atmosphere was more festive than concerned. People who didn't have cash couldn't get any because of course the ATMs didn't have any power. I saw the cashier accept checks and at least three foreign currencies. The young woman in front of me happened to be my neighbor from the apartment next to mine. She started laughing and then asked me to hold her place in line. "Sure," I said, "Did you forget something?" For an answer, she held out the packaged food that she had planned to buy. It was a microwave dinner, not helpful in a power blackout. Talk about disconnected! Later that night I walked to a friend's house and on the way saw a man unfolding a portable chair on a street corner. There were about 10 other people clustered around him, all staring up at the sky. "I didn't know the moon could be so bright," one of them said as I walked by.

On Ilha Grande several people talked about how it was easy to feel nourished by the spectacular nature around us there, but how hard it would be to keep that feeling alive back in the city. I disagreed. I live in the city, too, I thought, and under every square of asphalt is fertile soil. I drew a picture in my journal that week of a dandelion blooming from a crack in the pavement next to a subway entrance.

I'd thought that I wanted to bust out, change my life completely, say hasta luego to the city and the dance career that had been my life for almost 30 years. Instead, once I got back from Brazil, I wrote about the plants in the city and the burgeoning local food movement and the meals I shared with my friends when we gathered in my small home. I called my mom, my grandmother, and my dad and exchanged recipes with them long distance. I felt like I was on the trail of something important, but I didn't have a name for it yet.

Then I got the idea to do The 250, and instead of taking off for a year-long round-the-world trip I narrowed my world to just 250 miles in any direction from Park Slope, Brooklyn.

At the birthday party just before I started The 250, my friend Kendall gave me one of her enigmatic birthday cards. She is famous for these, and I always feel a little guilty when I give her a basic "Have a great year!" card on her birthday. There's just no matching her cards, so I don't even try. Kendall said she'd been thinking about what this local eating thing was really about for me, and she thought that once I made my home within the small circle of The 250 I would then be free to move away and move on. This is what she wrote:

"May this year bring you a million-mile radius of love and energy and possibility. May the roads open before you like magical carpets and transport you to wherever your heart desires. May you feel your own radius of influence and connection expand and extend. May you find a new sense of home that deepens as it widens."

I found her card encouraging. That's it! I thought. At the end of The 250 I'll finally feel at home here but also be free to let go and move on.

What I didn't count on was that I'd gone native. This California girl had grown fond of four seasons, even winter. I loved it that spring meant greens and garlic scapes and morel mushrooms, summer was tomatoes and eggplant and peaches, and just when I was sick of those there were the apples and leeks and carnival squashes of fall. I even grew attached to winter recipes that were dependent upon my "pantry": sauerkraut and apple salad, pasta sauces from my home-canned tomatoes, parsnips roasted in the homemade rosemary oil. Even before I was halfway through my 250-mile diet year, the lure of perpetual summer was not as attractive as it had been before I went to Ilha Grande.

I wanted to find out what this region tasted like. I didn't count on falling in love with it. I took a fresh look at my life, split between three careers I adore — dance, botany, and writing — and thought that if I met myself at a party and I was complaining, I'd probably punch me hard.

Up until that year I hadn't planted anything in my current garden that couldn't fulfill itself in one season. What was the point of a raspberry patch that wouldn't start bearing fruit until 2 years after I planted the canes? I wasn't sure I'd still be here in 2 years. But I decided that was beside the point. Someone else will enjoy the garden even after I've moved on. And the land on this patch of the planet is actually a little healthier and more fertile because I lived here and tended it. So I ordered five heritage-variety raspberry plants and planted them this spring. I still don't know that I'll be here when they eventually bear fruit. But I might be.

RECIPES FROM THE 250

Many of the recipes in this book were off limits to me during The 250. It was one thing to make rice pudding with coconut and bananas when I was in Brazil, quite another to make that same recipe in Brooklyn, where none of those things grow. Here are a few more recipes from The 250 just in case, like me, you live in a cold-winter climate and are trying to keep it local.

SPRING

Sorrel Soup
Serves 2, (recipe may be doubled)

The lemony tang of sorrel is especially welcome because I live in a climate where the winters are too harsh for lemons or any other citrus to grow. Sorrel grows as a weed in most temperate climates, but you can also buy plants and seeds. I sometimes see bunches of sorrel for sale at farmers markets. Sorrel contains oxalic acid, like spinach does, and should be an occasional treat rather than something you eat in quantity on a regular basis.

Sorrel goes beautifully with seafood, and I especially like sorrel soup made with fish stock.

> 1 pint fresh sorrel leaves, tough midribs removed, coarsely chopped
> 1½ tablespoons butter OR olive oil (whichever is your local lipid)
> 1 clove garlic, peeled and minced
> 1 large russet potato, peeled and cut into chunks
> 1 pint fish, chicken, or vegetable stock
> Salt
> 2 tablespoons sour cream or yogurt (optional)

1. Place the chopped sorrel leaves in a medium sized pot over medium-low heat with the butter. Stir constantly for a few minutes until the sorrel wilts and changes color from bright to drab green (an oxidation effect caused by the presence of oxalic acid). Proceed with Step 2 to make soup, or preserve for the winter by freezing (see instructions on the next page).

2. Add the garlic and stir for 30 seconds. Add the potatoes and stock and bring to a boil. Reduce heat and simmer until the potatoes are soft. Remove from heat.

3. For a rustic texture, use a potato masher to break up the potatoes. For a smoother soup, use an immersion blender to puree, or puree in a blender.

4. Return pot to stove over low heat. Add more stock if it seems too thick. Stir in salt to taste. Simmer for 5 minutes. Serve hot with a dollop of sour cream or yogurt, or chill for a cold soup in summer.

PRESERVING SORREL FOR WINTER SOUPS AND SAUCES

Proceed with Step 1 above. Spread the wilted sorrel and butter or oil into the bottom of a small (approximately 3-inch diameter) ramekin. Freeze for an hour. Immerse bottoms of ramekins in a bowl of very hot water for 30 seconds. Slide a butter knife around the sides of the sorrel butter. The sorrel butter will slip out as a solid disk. Sorrel butter disks will keep in the freezer for up to 6 months. Each disk will make one batch of soup, or can be used to make sauces for seafood.

SUMMER

The thing about summer is that you really don't need many recipes. A perfectly ripe tomato doesn't need anything but a little salt, and what is better than a beautifully sweet and juicy peach eaten as is? But sometimes summer's bounty overwhelms me with a surplus that I can't keep up with. Below is a recipe I use when my CSA farmer brings us a bumper crop of corn.

I've read that for the best corn-on-the-cob you need to start the water boiling before you go out to your corn patch to pick the corn. This is because the sugar in the kernels starts converting to starch the moment the corn is picked (though some recently developed super-sweet varieties hold their sugar a little longer than old-fashioned varieties). Since I don't have a corn patch, I am dependent for summer corn on what the farmers bring to my CSA and the farmers' markets. Even thought that is way tastier than corn that's been sitting on a supermarket shelf, it still isn't really "just picked." Nonetheless, when there is corn in my CSA share it pre-empts all other dinner plans so that I can eat at least one ear of corn while it is as fresh and sweet as possible. That leaves me with five or six additional ears. If I have the time and energy, I will blanch and freeze them that same night (instructions below). But sometimes a few ears of corn sit in my refrigerator for a few days before I can get around to them. This is an excellent recipe for getting the most out of corn that is a few days past when it was picked.

Third Day Corn
Serves 4

Fresh corn kernels sliced off 4 to 5 ears of corn (see tip below)
2 slices bacon
2 teaspoons butter
⅔ to 1 cup milk
A pinch of salt

1. Fry the bacon over medium-low heat in a heavy skillet until crispy, turning the slices over once while they cook. Drain the bacon on a paper towel. Pour fat out of pan (you can strain this through a coffee filter and use it for cooking if you aren't fat-phobic).

2. Melt the butter in the same pan over medium heat. Add the corn and cook, stirring often, 7 to 10 minutes, until the corn begins to brown.

3. Add the milk and the salt and bring to a simmer, stirring to release any yummy browned bits from the pan. Reduce the heat to medium-low and cook until the corn is tender and most of the milk has evaporated. If the milk is almost gone before the corn is tender, add a little more to prevent sticking.

4. Crumble the bacon and stir into the corn. Serve warm.

Tip: How to Slice Corn Kernels Off the Cob Without Having Them Fly All Over Your Apartment

Place a large mixing bowl, the largest one you've got, on a stable surface. Inside that bowl, place a smaller bowl upside down. Hold an ear of corn vertically with one end on the bottom of the upside down small bowl. With a sharp knife, slice downwards. The kernels bounce off the sides of the larger bowl and collect in the bottom without flying all over the place.

FREEZING CORN

Corn needs to be blanched before it is frozen. Get a big pot of water boiling while you husk the corn. Immerse the ears in the boiling water for 4 minutes. Remove and plunge into a big bowl of cold water until cooled. Use the method above to cut the kernels off the cob. Freeze the corn in freezer bags or containers for up to 8 months. If you blanch and freeze your corn while it is still very fresh it will retain most of its sweetness.

AUTUMN

I like to keep rosemary oil in my pantry at all times because it is so wonderful in so many things — roast chicken, roasted root vegetables, grilled zucchini and eggplant, even on popcorn. But I make at least two batches in the fall to last me through the winter because rosemary is not a reliably hardy plant in my climate. You could, of course, just buy a bundle of rosemary to use. My dad, in mild-wintered San Francisco, sneaks his from a neighbor's prolific patch of gorgeous trailing rosemary. I guess that could qualify as a kind of foraging.

ROSEMARY OIL

⅓ **cup fresh rosemary leaves, stripped from their woody stems**
1 cup extra-virgin olive oil

1. Put the rosemary and the oil into the insert of a slow-cooker. Cook uncovered on the high setting for 1 hour.

2. Remove insert from cooker and allow the oil to cool slightly. Strain through a coffee filter. Store in a glass bottle or jar at room temperature for up to 2 months or in the refrigerator for as long as 6 months.

WINTER

Here is a lovely, simple way to use the rosemary oil you made in the autumn. Almost any root vegetable will work but if you're using beets cook them separately or they'll turn your whole dish magenta. Young spring and summer turnips can be too watery and have a disappointing texture when roasted, but larger fall turnips work well. Potatoes, rutabagas, carrots, and parsnips are all excellent prepared this way.

Roasted Root Vegetables With Rosemary Oil

No amounts are given because you can make these in any sized batch from one potato for a solo dinner to several pounds to serve as a side dish for a crowd. Just be sure that you can spread them in a single layer when they go into the oven. If you have more than will fit in your pan, make more than one batch because piling them up prevents the yummy carmelization that you want the roots to get. For small batches I use my toaster oven.

Root vegetables, peeled and cut into approximately 1-inch chunks.
1 clove garlic per pound of roots, peeled and cut in half
Rosemary oil
Salt

1. Preheat oven to 400°F.

2. Toss the roots with enough rosemary oil to coat them in a shallow roasting pan. Sprinkle with salt.

3. Roast for 30 minutes, stirring twice during that time. Stir in the garlic. Roast for an addition 15 to 30 minutes, stirring occasionally, until the vegetables are browned but not burnt. Serve warm with additional salt if desired.

AND ONE MORE ... FOR ANY SEASON

Spicebush Ice Cream

1 pint heavy cream
1 pint milk
½ cup honey
¼ teaspoon salt
1 teaspoon ground spicebush berries (see Useful Resources Appendix for where to get these if you can't forage your own)
2 teaspoons vanilla extract (optional)

1. Over medium-low heat, bring 1 cup of the cream, the honey, and the salt to a simmer. Remove from heat and pour into a bowl.

2. Whisk in the remaining cup of cream, the milk, the ground spicebush, and the vanilla if using. Cover and refrigerate overnight or as long as 24 hours.

3. Pour the mixture into an ice cream machine and follow the machine manufacturer's instructions to freeze.

*Spicebush (*Lindera benzoin*)*

Afterword

❧ *Chocolate and Rutabagas* ❧

8:00 a.m. : Work on the latest edit of a *Pointe Magazine* review I wrote last week.

10:00 a.m.-

1:00 p.m. : Teach an herb gardening class at the Brooklyn Botanic Garden.

2:00 p.m. : While on the train into Manhattan, work on music and choreography notes for a new piece I start rehearsals for on Tuesday.

3:00 p.m.-

6:00 p.m. : Rehearsal for a ballet I'm restaging for Dances Patrelle. Subway nap on the way home.

7:30 p.m. :Write a new blog post with photos I took in the garden yesterday (perennials just waking up from their winter dormancy—first crocus bloom!).

8:30 p.m.:

Go into the kitchen to do something about dinner. Get excited when I remember that I have fresh salad greens. They arrived yesterday as part of the March delivery of my monthly CSA winter share. Lettuce and other tender greens mostly disappeared from my diet months ago when the season turned cold (I can't afford the pricy greenhouse salad mixes a few farmers offer all winter).

Get excited a second time when I remember that we also got rutabagas. I don't love rutabagas. I don't hate them either. It's a neutral relationship. Nonetheless, I am excited. I haven't tasted rutabagas yet this winter despite months of nothing much but root vegetables in the crisper drawers of my refrigerator. On a local, seasonal diet, each new taste is worth celebrating.

While rummaging for the rutabagas I find two disks of dark Venezuelan chocolate left over from the sugary haul I was given back in December. Concerned friends apparently thought that I would perish without cacao on my local foods diet. I rationed the chocolates, and did such a good job of it that I forgot about them. A plan for dinner takes shape in my mind: a fresh late-winter salad topped with some of the duck confit I made a few days ago, served hot on top of the cool greens; a rutabaga-apple bake alongside; South American chocolate for dessert.

As I tie on my apron and get the ingredients out of the refrigerator, I feel rich. I feel privileged. I guess I'm easy to please these days.

Rutabaga-Apple Bake
Serves 4

1 pound rutabagas, ends trimmed off, peeled
1 large apple, peeled and cored
2 tablespoons maple syrup
2 tablespoons butter
1 teaspoon salt
¼ teaspoon ground spicebush berries (see Useful Resources appendix) or black pepper

1. Preheat oven to 350°F.

2. Lightly grease a 6-to-8" casserole with butter

3. Shred the rutabagas using the wide holes of a box grater or the shredding blade of a food processor. Do the same with the apple, keeping it separate.

4. Combine the shredded rutabaga with the maple syrup, salt, ground spicebush or black pepper, and ¾ of the shredded apple. Scoop into the casserole. Top with the remaining apple.

5. Lightly press down on the shredded mixture to tamp into a fairly solid layer. Dot with the butter.

6. Bake, covered, for 1 hour. Uncover and bake for another 30 minutes or until the top is golden.

❧ Recipe Index ❧

❧ *Useful Resources* ❧

RECOMMENDED WEBSITES

The Forager's Feast
http://www.ledameredith.com
The blog that started with The 250 and is still where I report on my local food, foraging and gardening adventures.

Leda's Urban Homestead -
Video Channel http://youtube.com/ledameredith
Video tutorials about foraging for wild edible plants and mushroom, as well as food preservation techniques and recipes.

Backyard Forager
http://www.backyardforager.com/
Ellen Zachos' website with tips on foraging, gardening, and cooking.

Farm Aid
http://www.farmaid.org
Organization working to keep family farmers on their land.

Food Systems NYC
http://www.foodsystemsnyc.org
An organization working to increase access for all to safe and wholesome food, and to strengthen and expand the regional farm and food economy.

Forager's Harvest
http://www.foragersharvest.com/
Sam Thayer's wild food web site and also the place to buy his excellent wild edible plants book.

Grapestompers
http://grapestompers.com/
Home winemaking supplies including the fermentation locks I

mention in the Raspberry Cordial and Dandelion Wine recipes. Also acid titration kits for testing the acidity of homemade vinegars.

How to Test Homemade Vinegar
http://www.apple-cider-vinegar-benefits.com/vinegar-titration. html Clear instructions for using a wine-testing kit to find out if your homemade vinegar has a high enough acidity level to be safe to use in pickling.

Hunter, Angler, Gardener, Cook
http://honest-food.net/
Hank Shaw's award-winning work. His recipes and foraging instructions are completely trustworthy (and delicious).

Integration Acres
http://integrationacres.com
Mail-order source for wild spicebush berries in case you just gotta try that ice cream recipe but don't plan to go foraging. Note: Integration Acres sells spicebush (Lindera benzoin) as "Appalachian Allspice."

Just Food
http://www.justfood.org/
Comprehensive resources for finding, starting or managing a CSA in New York City. Just Food

Local Harvest
http://www.localharvest.org/csa
Local Harvest's site can help you locate CSAs and farmers' markets throughout the U.S.

Plants for a Future
http://www.pfaf.org
U.K. site that hosts a large database of information on edible and otherwise useful plants, including many wild ones. Includes tips on landscaping with edible plants.

Sourdough Home

http://www.sourdoughhome.com Everything sourdough, including recipes and how to make and maintain a starter.

Sustainable Table

http://sustainabletable.org Info and resources about the sustainable food movement.

The Meatrix

http://www.themeatrix.com Animated video about how the meat you eat is really raised and where to find better options.

Transitional Gastronomy

http://www.transitionalgastronomy.com/

If you are looking for culinary inspiration for foraged ingredients, what Pascal Bouder and Mia Wasilevich are doing will amaze you.

United Plant Savers

http://unitedplantsavers.org

An organization that works to protect native medicinal plants of the United States and Canada and their native habitat while ensuring an abundant renewable supply of medicinal plants for generations to come. You can order bare-root edible and medicinal woodland (think shade) plants from them.

Urban Sproule

http://urbansproule.com/

Locally harvested sea salt for those of you in the northeastern U.S.

Wild Food Adventures

http://wildfoodadventures.com/

John Kallas's site with information on wild food festivals and workshops nationwide.

Wild Food Plants

http://www.wildfoodplants.com

Sunny Savage's site. Includes very helpful and entertaining videos teaching identification, harvesting, and preparation techniques.

RECOMMEDED BOOKS

Northeast Foraging: 120 Wild and Flavorful Edibles from Beach Plums to Wineberries, Leda Meredith

Preserving Everything: Can, Culture, Pickle, Freeze, Ferment, Dehydrate, Salt, Smoke, and Store Fruits, Vegetables, Meat, Milk, and More, Leda Meredith

The Forager's Feast: How to Identify, Gather, and Prepare Wild Edibles, Leda Meredith

Animal, Vegetable, Miracle, Barbara Kingsolver

Backyard Foraging: 65 Familiar Plants You Didn't Know You Could Eat, Ellen Zachos

Coming Home to Eat: The Pleasures and Politics of Local Food, Gary Paul Nabhan

In Defense of Food: An Eater's Manifesto, Michael Pollan

Making Wild Wines and Meads: 125 Unusual Recipes Using Herbs, Fruits, Flowers and More, Pattie Vargas and Rich Gulling

My Side of the Mountain, Jean Craighead George

Nourishing Traditions: The Cookbook that Challenges Politically Correct Nutrition and the Diet Dictocrats, Sally Fallon

Plenty: One Man, One Woman, and a Raucous Year of Eating Locally, Alisa Smith & J.B. Mackinnon

Hunt, Gather, Cook: Finding the Forgotten Feast, Hank Shaw

Preserving Food without Freezing or Canning: Traditional Techniques Using Salt, Oil, Sugar, Alcohol, Vinegar, Drying, Cold Storage, and Lactic Fermentation, The Gardeners and Farmers of Terre Vivant

Putting Food By, Janet Greene

The Audobon Guide to Mushrooms, Gary Lincoff

The Forager's Harvest, Sam Thayer

The Joy of Foraging, Gary Lincoff

The New Wildcrafted Cuisine: Exploring the Exotic Gastronomy of Local Terroir, Pascal Baudar

The Omnivore's Dilemma: A Natural History of Four Meals, Michael Pollan

The Revolution Will Not Be Microwaved, Sandor Katz

Wild Fermentation, Sandor Katz

DANCE

Dance companies and schools mentioned in this book:

American Ballet Theatre http://www.abt.org

Dances Patrelle http://www.dancespatrelle.org

Jennifer Muller/The Works http://www.jmtw.org

Dance Loft Switzerland CSDP http://danceloft.ch

❧ *Acknowledgements* ❧

Thanks to:

My husband and best friend, Richard Orbach. You are probably right about the moon.

Life coach Meike Fruchtenicht, health counselor Jena La Flamme, and the rest of the Brazil gang for getting it started.

Naomi Rosenblatt, Michael Fancello, Gerry Daly, Anne Finkelstein and everyone at Heliotrope Books for making it real. Sally Pope for her editorial help and encouragement.

Those who read early incarnations of the original edition, listened to readings, and tested recipes: Cynthia Gregory, Sean Berry, Jenny Giering, Valerie Vigoda, Erica Marks Panush, The Guinea Pig for UHN, Bill Hedberg, Phyllis Hedberg, Ellen Zachos, Michael Macdonald, Kim Carlson, Janice Novet, Rita Watson, and especially Kelly Johnson and Penelope and Frank Coberly. And to culinary goddess Mia Wasilevich for reading the rough draft of this new edition.

Everyone at the Park Slope CSA: I miss you!

Jennifer Muller and Francis Patrelle for their ongoing support of my dance career in all of its incarnations.

Melina Hammer and Eduardo Patino for the photos.

Eugenia Kilgore a.k.a. Grandma Nea, Jody White, G.T., and Ella, who are still with me in spirit.

And to all the gardens, both wild and tamed, for reminding me what matters.

❧ *About the Author* ❧

A lifelong forager (it's her great-grandmother's fault), Leda Meredith is the author of five books including *The Forager's Feast: How to Identify, Gather, and Prepare Wild Edibles*, *The Locavore's Handbook: the Busy Person's Guide to Eating Local on a Budget*, and *Northeast Foraging: 120 Wild and Flavorful Edibles from Beach Plums to Wineberries*.

She has a certification in Ethnobotany and is an instructor at the New York Botanical Garden and at the Brooklyn Botanic Garden. She is the winner of a Teaching Excellence award from Adelphi University. Leda was a professional dancer for over thirty years with companies including San Francisco Opera Ballet, American Ballet Theater II, Dances Patrelle, and Jennifer Muller/The Works, among many others. She continues to teach, direct, and choreograph dance internationally. You can find out more about what she's up to on her website at www.ledameredith.com

Leda in the kitchen
Photo by Melina Hammer

CPSIA information can be obtained
at www.ICGtesting.com
Printed in the USA
LVHW051348210520
656048LV00002B/240